2019 EDITION

iPhone®

MADE EASY

This is a **FLAME TREE** book
First published 2015

Publisher and Creative Director: Nick Wells
Commissioning Editor: Polly Prior
Senior Project Editor: Josie Mitchell
Art Director and Layout Design: Mike Spender
Digital Design and Production: Chris Herbert
Copy Editor: Daniela Nava
Technical Editor: Mark Mayne
Screenshots: Chris Smith

Special thanks to: Helen Snaith and Dawn Laker.

This edition first published 2015 by
FLAME TREE PUBLISHING
6 Melbray Mews, London SW6 3NS
United Kingdom

www.flametreepublishing.com

19 21 23 22 20
1 3 5 7 9 10 8 6 4 2

© 2019 Flame Tree Publishing

ISBN 978-1-78755-272-2

Printed in China

All non-screenshot pictures are © 2019 Apple Inc.: 1, 3, 8, 9, 10, 18, 21, 60, 154, 196, 224; and imore.com: 25; and © copyright
Libratone 2019: 197; and iStock and © the following photographers: pressureUA: 5, 94; Erikona: 5, 54; georgeclerk: 6, 166; Onfokus: 6,
150; BlueMoonPics: 20, 208; tamergunal: 22; CatLane: 164; and Shutterstock and © the following photographers: Denys Prykhodov:
4, 7, 12, 16, 25, 126, 132, 218; successo images: 9; Ostancov Vladislav: 18; Oleg GawriloFF: 19, 77; guteksk7: 21; NorGal: 24; Leszek
Kobusinski: 31; ymgerman: 41; nenetus: 47; hitmanphoto: 50; Sebastian Gauert: 73; Zeynep Demir: 80, 81; tulpahn: 100; Chukcha: 114;
Halfpoint: 129; Pressmaster: 156; leonardo2011 159; blvdone: 163; alexisdc: 185; eljkodan: 192; guteksk7: 230; Valentin Valkov: 234;
Hadrian: 246. All other images courtesy of Flame Tree Publishing Ltd.

2019 EDITION

iPhone®
MADE EASY

KIERAN ALGER AND CHRIS SMITH

FLAME TREE
PUBLISHING

CONTENTS

It's often difficult to know where to start if you have never used an iPhone before. This chapter will introduce what you can accomplish with your new smartphone; it will also furnish you with the knowledge needed to get past the initial setup process and to get comfortable with the device. You'll become accustomed to using the touch screen, moving around the iOS software, opening apps and accessing some of the iPhone's basic features.

USING THE iPHONE

Although the iPhone is a multifunctional device, harnessing the power of several gadgets rolled into one, at its core it is still a communications tool. This chapter offers a comprehensive guide to making and receiving phone calls, setting up voicemail, importing your contacts, sending and receiving text and picture messages, and even video chatting with your friends and family.

GETTING CONNECTED

With the iPhone, the entire world is in your pocket. In this chapter, you'll learn how to browse the internet using the Safari app, send and receive email, control your calendar, and post updates to Facebook and Twitter. This chapter will also explain in foolproof detail how to use the iPhone's powerful location services, which allow you to summon directions instantly, check in at your favourite restaurant, find nearby attractions and explore cities new and old.

Even if you are a smartphone novice, you willl have heard of the mobile apps phenomenon pioneered by the iPhone. In this chapter we'll learn how to download and make use of these new and exciting tools from the App Store and we'll discover how they can be used to keep your iPhone feeling fresh and new.

Did you know that your new iPhone is also a camera, camcorder, portable games console, portable music and video player, digital book, personal trainer and more? This chapter

features a comprehensive guide to taking great pictures and video, and sharing them with your friends and family; we'll also explore how to acquire and play your favourite games, music, movies and TV shows, how to read your limitless books and magazines, and how to improve your lifestyle through a host of dedicated apps and services.

ADVANCED iPHONE

Before you know it, you'll be ready to shed that 'iPhone beginner' tag and move on to some of the iPhone's more advanced functionality. Need to restore from a backup? Improve your battery life? Make use of online file storage apps? It's all here. This chapter also features a detailed troubleshooting guide to counter some of the common problems you'll come across when using your iPhone.

INTRODUCTION

As you're reading this, you've probably just become the lucky owner of a brand new iPhone. Now you may be wondering 'Where do I start?' You've come to the right place. This book offers both a practical and educational guide to quickly mastering this pocket-size marvel of modern technology.

Above: The iPhone is many devices rolled into one, plus so much more.

WHAT CAN I DO WITH AN iPHONE?

The iPhone boasts an incredible number of practical everyday uses for personal and business use. It encompasses a multitude of modern devices but is still small enough to fit in the palm of your hand. It's a phone, a personal organizer, a music and video player, a camera and so much more. This book will help you to master simple tasks, such as making phone calls and sending emails, to more complex tasks, such as taking photos, using apps to edit them and then logging on to the internet in order to upload them to your favourite social networks.

A QUICK iPHONE HISTORY LESSON

There have now been 21 versions of the iPhone with at least two new models (bringing additional features and improved software) now arriving each year. Some of the features only apply to newer or older handsets, and we'll make that clear throughout this book. Here's a brief guide to the features and improvements each handset offered down the years.

iPhone Models

Here's a summary of each new iPhone to date:

- **iPhone (2007):** Apple 'reinvented the phone', creating a new mobile operating system to fit a 3.5-inch, touchscreen device. It had a web browser, an iPod MP3 player, a video player and apps such as Weather, Calendar and Google Maps.

- **iPhone 3G (2008)/iPhone 3GS (2009):** Better, 3G internet, and better GPS. The App Store was also introduced, bringing new web-based applications and games.

- **iPhone 4 (2010)/iPhone 4S (2011):** A critically acclaimed stainless-steel and glass design, a 5-megapixel camera, a front-facing camera for video calls and the new high-resolution Retina display. The 4S introduced Siri – a voice controlled assistant – and an online back-up solution, iCloud. It had an 8-megapixel camera with HD video recording.

- **iPhone 5 (2012)/iPhone 5S and 5C (2013):** A larger 4-inch screen, more power, better graphics, fourth generation mobile internet (4G LTE), a new charging connector and iOS 6 software. Apple added the Touch ID fingerprint sensor to the 5S, improving security. It shipped with iOS 7, the biggest software overhaul since the first iPhone.

- **iPhone 6 and 6 Plus (2014):** With a design overhaul and a larger screen, the iPhone 6 got slimmer, lighter and rounder integrating a 4.7-inch screen. iOS 8 also arrived with this handset. The 6 Plus is the largest handset so far, at 5.5 inches; it is also the first iPhone to boast a full HD 1080p screen.

- **iPhone 6 and 6S Plus (2015):** No design or screen changes here, but

Right: Side view of the sleek iPhone 5S.

Apple added new hardware features like 3D Touch and Live Photos. This handset shipped with iOS 9.

- **iPhone SE (2016):** A 4-inch display size, but included the power of the iPhone 6.

- **iPhone 7 and 7 Plus (2016):** The very latest models got rid of the headphone socket. The iPhone 7S Plus also has two camera lenses. The 2017 iPhone 8 and 8 Plus were similar and the last to feature a Home button.

- **iPhone 8 and 8 Plus (2017):** Similar to the iPhone 7 range, and the last to feature a Home button. They also introduced wireless charging capabilities.

- **iPhone X (2017):** No Home button, a full screen design and the Face ID sensor, which replaced Touch ID. It arrived with iOS 11.

- **iPhone XS, iPhone XS Max (2018):** The latest and greatest iPhones, they have 5.8-inch and 6.5-inch screens respectively. The XS Max is the largest ever iPhone. These arrived with iOS 12.

- **iPhone XR (2018):** Full screen phone, like the iPhone X, but a more affordable build and with six different colour finishes.

Apple iOS Software

You'll read a lot about iOS in this book: it's the software that comes pre-loaded on to the iPhone for use straight out of the box. The latest

Above: The iPhone XS is one of the latest models of iPhone. It arrived with iOS 12.

version is iOS 12, which the majority of iPhone owners are now using, while almost all of the rest are on iOS 11. Apple's improvements to its iPhone handsets each year are always accompanied by a tweaked version of iOS but even if you're using an older phone (iPhone 5S and up), you can still upgrade to the new software every time. When certain features are only available in iOS 12, we'll make that clear.

DIVE IN AND DIVE OUT

This book has been written in the hope that you will dive in and out when you need a helping hand to understand a particular feature or if you're having trouble overcoming a problem. For example, if you don't know how to stream from Apple Music, or email a picture, you can head straight to that page for a detailed explanation. If you're stumped, the easiest thing to do is to look up your topic in the index page.

JARGON BUSTING

While we have made every effort to crush buzzwords and display instructions in the simplest possible terms, sometimes jargon is unavoidable (iTunes Syncing, 3D Touch, etc.).

HELP!

We are confident that the information within this book can help you to become fluent in the language of the iPhone. But if you need further advice, the Apple Support website offers hugely detailed archives on how to master each feature and overcome problems.

Above: The book contains useful screenshots that help you understand what is being explained.

Hot Tips

Throughout the book, we have inserted a host of Hot Tips to help you get the most out of your iPhone. These simple features can be less obvious or hidden away, but can provide the key to unlocking more cool features on your iPhone handset.

WHAT IS AN iPHONE?

An iPhone is a mobile phone with software that lets users search the internet, send email, play music, video and games, take photos, shoot video and find directions. Here, we'll introduce some of the key uses for your new iPhone: there are more than you think!

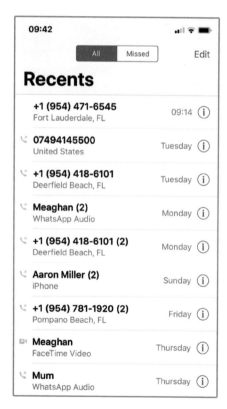

Above: Once an active SIM card has been installed, the iPhone can be used to make and receive calls.

COMMUNICATION

Multi-talented the iPhone may be, but its primary function is still communication. Here are some of the ways you can use it to keep in touch directly with friends and family; all will be explained in more detail throughout this book.

Phone

Once an active SIM card is placed in the device, you'll be able to make and receive calls by pressing the Phone icon on the device's Home screen and using the onscreen dial pad.

Messaging

The SMS (short message service) or 'texting' app is a primary function of the iPhone. Messages are typed on the touch-screen keypad and, once sent, will appear in a thread, allowing you to keep track of conversations over time. iPhone, iPad, Mac and iPod touch owners can exchange messages with each other for free over Wi-Fi or mobile internet using Apple's own iMessage service.

Email

The iPhone's native email app allows you to send and receive electronic mail directly to your handset; it's easy to configure your Google Mail, Yahoo! Mail, Microsoft Outlook and more. Microsoft Exchange users can also have their work emails sent straight to the device and we'll explain exactly how to do this in the Getting Connected chapter (*see* pages 94–149).

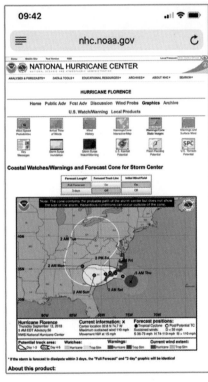

Above: iPhone's Safari browser allows you to access websites on the internet.

FaceTime

FaceTime is an Apple-to-Apple free video chat app which uses the front-facing camera. You can also make FaceTime Audio calls, meaning you can contact anyone using an iPhone, iPad or iPod touch (or Mac computer) using Wi-Fi or mobile data. In iOS 12 you can make group video calls with up to 32 people.

INTERNET

The iPhone is the entire internet in your pocket and can be accessed through apps or the built-in Safari browser.

App Store

Each icon on your iPhone's Home screen is an app (Mail, Phone, etc.), but there are thousands more of these self-contained applications in the App Store. They are a great way to keep your phone fresh with exciting new content.

Maps

The iPhone has a built-in Maps application made by Apple. It allows users to search for directions, but can also replace your sat nav unit with its voice-guided, turn-by-turn navigation feature.

MULTIMEDIA

The iPhone is also a full-on personal media player and games console packed into a pocket-size device. We'll be going into greater detail on all of these features throughout this guide.

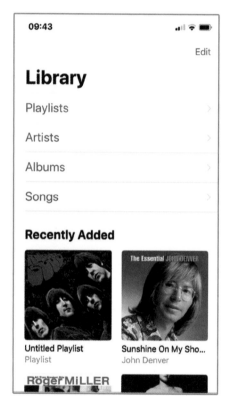

Above: The Music app is incorporated into the iPhone, allowing you to stream music on the go.

Music

There are many ways to enjoy music on your iPhone. You can transfer and store your digital music collection on it, or you can sign up for Apple Music (and other streaming services). These offer unlimited access to millions of tracks for £9.99/$9.99 a month. Or you can buy tracks outright on the iTunes store.

Video

You can also stream from apps like Netflix or rent or buy the latest movies and TV shows from the iTunes app. As with music, you can also transfer your favourite digital movies and TV shows on to the iPhone for small screen playback.

Games

The iPhone has become a popular gaming device thanks to addictive games like Candy Crush, Minecraft and Pokémon Go. Old favourites, such as Scrabble and Monopoly and mobile versions of console games can also be downloaded.

that is the same thing. See!" she contin-
ued, pointing to the corner of the
house. "There are her two feet, still
sticking out from under a block of
wood."

Dorothy looked, and gave a little
cry of fright. There, indeed, just under
the corner of the great beam the house
rested on, two feet were sticking out,
shod in silver shoes with pointed toes.

"Oh, dear! Oh, dear!" cried
Dorothy, clasping her hands together in
dismay. "The house must have fallen on
her. Whatever shall we do?"

"There is nothing to be done," said
the little woman calmly.

"But who was she?" asked Dorothy.

"She was the Wicked Witch of the
East, as I said," answered the little
woman. "She has held all the
Munchkins in bondage for many years,
making them slave for her night and

Above: The Apple Books app allows you to access a
bookstore through which millions of titles can be purchased,
downloaded and read on your iPhone.

Hot Tip

Use the Photo Library portion
of iCloud to save your photos
online automatically.

Books

Apple offers an app and accompanying bookstore
(Apple Books – *see* page 206) that allows access
to 2.5 million books, available to download and be
read directly on the iPhone.

CAMERA

The camera on more recent
iPhone models is so good
that you can probably start
leaving your trusty compact
camera or camcorder at
home on most occasions and
not worry about precious
memories being tinged by
terrible photos.

Photography

The stills camera has got progressively better since
it was an afterthought on the first iPhone. It has
increasingly become a major selling point for the
phone. Quality improves each year, with models
from the iPhone 7 and 7 Plus offering two rear-
facing cameras and an excellent 'selfie' cam.

Video Camera

The video camera on the iPhone 6S and up allows
users to record video at 4K, the same as most video
cameras on the market. Older handsets shoot at
1080p HD, which is the same as most TV shows.

ANATOMY OF AN iPHONE

The new iPhone XS and XS Max arguably represent the pinnacle of modern mobile technology. In this section, we'll explain some of the design intricacies, the features and the functions of the physical buttons and switches. But first, let's crack open the packaging.

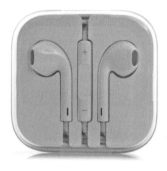

Above: The Apple EarPods headphones, with volume controls seen in the center.

Left:
The headphone adapter makes it possible to use wired headphones with the iPhone 7 range, which does not have the traditional jack.

WHAT'S IN THE BOX?

Within that minimalist packaging is everything you'll need to harness that new smartphone sitting invitingly within the box.

Earphones

Apple gives you a free pair of earphones with every iPhone called EarPods. They're designed to fit the ear canal well, while also featuring a microphone and volume controls.

Headphone Adapter

Apple ditched the 3.5 mm headphone jack with the iPhone 7 and iPhone 7S. So, to use the bundled AirPods, you'll plug them into the charging port or – with older headphones – use a little adapter that plugs into the charging port.

Charger and Cable

With moderate use the iPhone's battery should last a day, but then will need charging. The charging cable slots into the mains adapter and the bottom of the iPhone. It can also be plugged into the USB port on your computer to charge, sync or transfer content between the latter and your iPhone (see page 20). Newer iPhones can be wirelessly charged.

iPHONE EXPLAINED: BUTTONS

Although most of your activities will be conducted via the touch screen (opening apps, typing, taking photos, playing music), the iPhone still has a few essential buttons and switches:

1 Power Button

Holding down this button – positioned on the right-hand side (and on the top of older devices) – for a moment will allow you to switch your iPhone on and off. Pressing it once will wake the screen from its slumber.

Volume keys **3**

Mute switch **4**

Speakers **7**

Connector port **6**

Power button **1**

Headphone jack **5**

Home button **2**

2 Home Button

The four newest iPhones, X/XS/XS Max and XR, don't have a home button, and we'll explain more on that soon. For older phones, pressing the home button will always bring you back to your Home screen. Pressing it when the device is asleep will wake up the screen; pressing it twice in quick succession will launch the multitasking bar, allowing you to switch between apps, whereas holding it down for a second will launch Siri (iPhone 4S and up). On all handsets from the iPhone 5S to the iPhone 8/8 Plus, the Home button also houses the Touch ID

fingerprint sensor, which allows authorized users to unlock the
phone and make payments. The iPhone X and 2018 iPhones
use a new Face ID facial recognition technology (*see* page 27).

Hot Tip

**The volume buttons
can also be used to
trigger the camera
(*see* page 17).**

❸ Volume Keys

The two volume buttons are on the left side and
allow you to adjust the volume of calls and media.

❹ Mute Switch

There are few things more embarrassing than your Star Wars ringtone blaring during an
important meeting. You can quickly curtail 'The Imperial March' by flicking the Mute switch.

❺ Headphone Jack

Apple killed this with the iPhone 7/7 Plus, but on earlier models there's a headphone jack on
the bottom. You can use this to plug in the bundled-in earphones,
your own set or any speaker that has a 3.5 mm cable.

❻ Connector Port

The 'Lightning' connector at the bottom of the device
allows you to charge your iPhone's battery, and to plug it
into your computer to transfer content and synchronize
important data.

❼ Speakers

There are two speakers. The first is in the earpiece,
which allows you to hear calls. On newer iPhones
(iPhone 7/Plus and up) this acts as a loud-speaker
enabling surround-sound like effects. The second,
more powerful speaker on the bottom of the device
plays music and other audio (*see* image on page 19).

OTHER PHYSICAL CHARACTERISTICS

1 **Screen**

There is a now wide range of iPhone screen sizes. The 2018 models have 5.8-inch, 6.1-inch and 6.5-inch options, the latter of which is the largest iPhone ever. However, the iPhone 6/6S/7/8 have a 4.7-inch screen; while the iPhone 6 Plus/6S Plus/7Plus/8 Plus are 5.5 inches. Larger screens mean widescreen video and room for more apps. If you want a really pocket-friendly device, track down an iPhone SE, which has a 4-inch screen.

Rear Camera **4**

Flash

ar Camera

FaceTime Camera **3**

9:48

Wednesday, November 15

Screen **1**

Retina Display **2**

iPhone

❷ Retina Display

iPhones feature Apple's Retina Display technology, meaning photos, text and videos appear much clearer to the eye (these screens have more pixels than the human eye can distinguish when the phone is held at arm's length).

❸ FaceTime Camera

The front-facing camera enables video calls over its FaceTime app (see page 15) and selfies. On newer models it also allows Face ID to unlock the phone.

❹ Rear Camera

The back of an iPhone features a lens, which is much smaller than the one in a compact camera, and appears in the top-left corner of the device. There's also a flash sitting next to the lens. On the higher-end iPhones like the iPhone XS Max there are two camera lenses.

Use Protection!

The iPhone isn't a cheap piece of kit to replace. To help keep it pristine, we'd suggest buying a case to safeguard it against drops, and a screen protector to guard against scratches and scuffs.

Hot Tip

The camera flash can also be used as a torch. Access the Control Center and select the flashlight icon.

INSIDE YOUR iPHONE

The iPhone looks pretty, but the magic is created inside, as each generation becomes more powerful. Below is a list of some of the internal features.

- **Processor:** The newest and best iPhones feature the Apple A12 Bionic processor, which makes them the fastest and most powerful yet.

- **Storage:** The newest iPhone models now offer three storage options: 64 GB, 256 GB and 512GB. Older models have widely varying storage options.

- **Battery:** The iPhone's battery is not removable. As the phone ages, you may need to take it to the Apple Store (or an authorised third-party) to be replaced.

- **Wi-Fi:** Providing you have the password, this allows you to connect to any wireless network and access internet-based content.

- **Mobile internet:** The iPhone has mobile data connectivity that allows you to access the internet on the go. Your mobile network (O2, EE, etc.) will place a limit on how much data you can use each month as part of your contract.

- **Bluetooth:** Bluetooth is one of the best ways of sharing photos or connecting to other devices. Use Bluetooth speakers to play music wirelessly on your iPhone. The newer iPhones contain Bluetooth 5 technology, which causes low strain on the battery and works over greater distances.

- **GPS:** The chip inside your iPhone allows satellites to pinpoint your location and use mapping services.

- **NFC:** The iPhone 6 and up have a built-in Near-Field Communications chip for Apple Pay. You can pay for goods and services in the same way you use a contactless debit card.

- **W1 Chip:** From the iPhone 7, Apple included a chip for quick connection to its AirPods.

GETTING STARTED

Now we're familiar with the iPhone, both inside and out, it's almost time to push that Power button for the first time. In this section, we'll get you past all of the tedious pre-use steps and setup screens.

Above: All iPhone models since 2012 require a nano-SIM, but older ones use a slightly larger micro-SIM.

THE SIM CARD

If this is your first iPhone, you'll almost certainly need a new SIM card. This card has a chip containing all your personal information and communicates with your mobile network. The iPhone requires a nano-SIM (unless it's an iPhone 4S or older, they have a MicroSIM).

Activating the New SIM Card

When you purchase your iPhone, you may be provided with a new SIM card or you may choose to use your old one so that you keep your the same phone number. In the former case, your network should take care of transferring your current phone number and details over to a new SIM, allowing you to just insert-and-go. In some circumstances, it may be necessary to call the network to activate the new SIM. They may ask for the SIM card number and iPhone serial number.

Hot Tip

If you insert the SIM and then receive an 'activation failed' message onscreen, you'll know it hasn't been activated yet. Call your network: it'll take minutes to fix.

Inserting the SIM Card

As with SIM activation, if you have bought or intend to buy the iPhone in-store, then the staff there will be more than happy to help you through these steps:

1. Place the SIM tray eject tool (or a bent paperclip) into the pinhole on the right side of the device.

2. Slowly withdraw the pin to release the SIM tray.

3. Remove the SIM card from its plastic housing and place the SIM card into the SIM tray so the chip faces down.

4. Carefully replace the SIM tray until it's firmly closed.

Above: Use a paperclip or eject tool, as shown here, to release the SIM tray.

POWER UP

Out of the box, the iPhone arrives with a moderate amount of battery charge. Simply hold down the Power button on top, or the side, of the phone, for a second and you'll see the Apple logo, which stays in place for about 10 seconds.

SETTING UP YOUR iPHONE

Once the Apple logo disappears, you'll see a Hello screen. Tap the Home button to enter the Set-Up Assistant. In the following pages there are some step-by-step guides to each of the screens you'll encounter. Depending on the iPhone model/version of iOS you're using, these may be in a slightly different order or with slightly different options.

Above: When you first turn on your new iPhone, you will be greeted with the iPhone setup screen.

Above: Scroll down to select your country of residence and then press 'Next' in the top right-hand corner of the screen.

Above: You can select a Wi-Fi network and enter the password. This will then become the default source of internet whenever possible.

Language and Country

The first two screens ask you to select your language and country of residence. English is selected as default. On the Country or Region screen, use a finger to scroll down to your country and repeat.

Quick Start

If you have another Apple device running iOS 12 (like an iPad), you can perform the Quick Start to breeze through set-up. Just bring the two devices close together when you see the Quick Start screen.

Choose a Wi-Fi Network

The iPhone will ask you to configure a Wi-Fi network to activate your phone. You can use mobile data, but we'd recommend taking the Wi-Fi route.

1. The screen will display available Wi-Fi networks and their respective signal strengths. Those which have a padlock icon next to the signal indicator mean that you'll need a password for access.

2. Touch the network of your choice. It'll either be named after a place (e.g. Starbucks) or retain the name written on the router (e.g. NETGEAR ZW52).

3. Enter the password, which will also be written on your Wi-Fi router, by typing it in using the keyboard.

4. Press Join to move on to the next screen.

Location Services

Next, you'll be asked whether you'd like to enable Location Services. This is important if you'd like to use the Maps app, or to use apps that rely on knowing your location. It can also be used to 'geo-tag' photos and social networking posts.

Touch ID and Face ID

Next you'll decide how to keep your iPhone secure. On iPhones with a Home button you'll need to configure the Touch ID sensor. For newer iPhones without the Home button it's Face ID. Follow the instructions on screen. Once complete, this can be used to unlock the phone, confirm app purchases and more.

Passcode

Enter a six-digit password, which is needed to access your phone when locked. Don't make the passcode something too obvious, like your date of birth.

Apps & Data

The next screen is important as it details how you'll set up your phone. You can restore from an old iCloud Backup or Restore from iTunes Backup. These are great options if you've owned an iPhone before or need to restore the device. If this is your first iPhone, choose 'Set-up as a new iPhone'. If you're choosing this, jump to the section on setting up your Apple ID below.

Moving from Android?

The final option on the Apps & Data screen is 'Move Data from Android'. This is a fantastic way to seamlessly move content, photos, personal data and apps over from a Samsung, HTC or

20:42

Cancel

Move your head slowly to complete the circle.

Above: Registering your face with Face ID adds an extra level of security and is safer than a fingerprint.

Motorola device (and countless others too!). It takes a bit of back and forth, but here's how to do it:

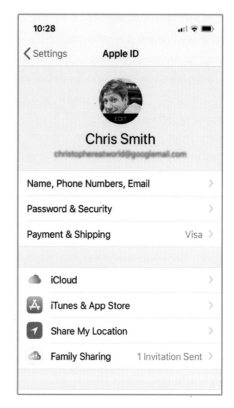

1. Select Move Data From Android on your iPhone.

2. On your old phone install the Move to iOS app from the Google Play Store. Open it, agree to terms, tap next and then select Find Your Code.

3. On your new iPhone, tap Continue and wait for the 10-digit code to appear. Enter the code on your Android device.

4. Next you'll see a Transfer Data screen on the Android device. Select everything you want to send to your iPhone.

Apple ID

Regardless of which of the last options you selected, the next step is to set up the Apple ID. This allows you to download apps, purchase media, sync your accounts and much more. If you have an Apple ID, insert the username and password here.

Above: Set up your Apple ID to start accessing the App Store, iCloud and iTunes.

If not, you can easily set up a free account. You'll need to insert a valid email address, a strong password and your date of birth. Next you'll need to answer three security questions and add a rescue email address. Finally, you will need to agree to the Apple's terms and conditions.

Siri

Next you'll be asked to set up Siri, the voice-powered personal assistant. It's not necessary, but it's at least worth your time to give Siri a chance to impress you. During this step, you'll be asked to speak some phrases so Siri gets to know your voice. If Siri has trouble understanding you, it may be your accent. Go to Settings > General > Siri > Language to select English (UK) or English (US).

iCloud

iCloud is Apple's free online storage and backup service. Its most basic function is to ensure that your contacts, documents, photos, mail and calendar are saved on servers in case your device is lost or stolen. It's great for remembering the apps, music, books and video you've purchased from iTunes and allowing you to re-download them at your convenience. Beyond that, there are two further facets; iCloud Keychain (which is a great option for storing all of your online passwords across devices) and iCloud Drive, which enables you to sync files from your iPhone and make them available online (see Advanced iPhone, page 218).

Above: When setting up your iPhone, you'll be asked to enable Siri, which is a voice-controlled personal assistant.

Apple Pay

Apple Pay allows you to use your phone as a contactless payment method in the same way you'll probably already do with your contactless card. When you tap your phone on the card receiver, it'll send a one-time code to the retailer, and you'll authenticate the purchase with your Touch ID fingerprint. It can also be used to make payments on the web or within apps so you don't have to input your card details. With a new iPhone you'll be asked to set up Apple Pay during set-up:

1. When you agree to add Apple Pay, the camera interface will open and you can capture the card details by lining it up within the frame. You can also do this manually.

2. You'll need to confirm the security code and the expiry date and then agree to the terms.

3. Next you'll need to verify the addition with your bank.

4. Once this is complete, you'll be able to hold your phone next to the reader and the card you've added will pop up.

Customise the Click (iPhone 7 and 8)

The Home button had lost its 'click' with the iPhone 7 and 8 ranges, the last iPhones with Home buttons. Here you can customise the 'click'. If you have an iPhone X or newer, you can learn about gestures you'll use instead of the Home button (*see page 34*).

Other Setup Options

Depending on your device, you may be asked to configure:

- **True Tone display**: Enabling this will automatically adjust the colour and the intensity of the display to make images look more natural.

- **Find My iPhone**: Allows you to track down a lost iPhone.

- **Diagnostics**: Agreeing to this will send feedback to app developers based on your usage habits.

Above: Adding your card details to Apple Pay means you'll be able to use your phone to complete transactions at thousands of shops.

Setup Complete

There's so much more still to setup, such as your email and social networks, as well as finding and downloading all the apps you'd like, but these will be tackled later in the book. For now, let's explore your new iPhone.

iPHONE BASICS

Over the course of the next few pages, we'll offer some basic tips on familiarizing yourself with the Home screen, moving around the device, using the touch screen, typing on the keyboard and more.

THE iPHONE

The screenshot on the right illustrates the iPhone's Home screen after you've first set up the device; below are some of the key elements to take note of.

1 **iPhone Title Bar**

The iPhone title bar features many vital indicators, described here from left to right.

2 **Time**: Displays the current time. When the phone is locked you'll see the network identity (O2, Vodafone, Three, etc.).

3 **Signal Strength**: The more bars you see, the stronger your mobile signal. This affects your ability to make clear voice calls and send texts.

4 **Internet**: If you're connected to Wi-Fi, you'll see the fan icon. Once again, the fullness of the fan represents the strength of the signal. If you're using mobile internet, you'll usually see the letters 3G, 4G or LTE. If there's zero connectivity, nothing is displayed.

Time   Location   Signal strength   Internet   Battery

2   6   3   4   5

1   Title bar

Above: The iPhone X's Home screen in iOS 12.

Airplane Mode   Clock   Headphones   Battery

④   ①   ②   ③

Above: Title bar icons as seen in the Control Center.

⑤ Battery: This shows how much battery you've used. Once you get to 20 per cent or lower, it will turn red or yellow if you enable a 'Low Power Mode.'

⑥ Location: If you're using Maps or your iPhone is scanning for your location, the compass arrow will appear.

Other Title Bar Indicators

Here are some further indicators that may appear within the title bar, depending on what's running on the iPhone. If you have an iPhone X or newer, many of these will only appear in the title bar when you're viewing the Control Center screen.

① Clock: If you've set an alarm, a stopwatch or a timer, a clock icon will be present.

② Headphones: If you have headphones or a Bluetooth speaker connected you'll see it indicated, along with an icon representing the remaining battery on that pair of headphones.

③ Battery: The remaining battery life presented as a percentage.

④ Airplane: If you have enabled Airplane Mode, which disables cellular connectivity while still allowing you to use other features when flying, a plane icon will appear.

APP ICONS

The iPhone's Home screen is taken up by rows of apps.

Dock

This is at the foot of the Home screen and maintains the same four icons at all times. The idea is to include the apps that you use most, to make them more accessible. The apps that appear by default are Phone, Mail, Safari and Music.

App Folders

Like-minded apps can be placed in Folders under names like Utilities. This makes the phone easier to navigate. Drag one app on to another to create a new folder, and give it a name.

Multiple Home Screens

The iPhone arrives with two screens of apps, but when they're full, more will open up. To move between them, swipe left or right across the screen. The white dots above the dock indicate which screen you are currently on.

Today Screen

Swiping to the left from the Home or lock screen reveals a 'Today' screen featuring Spotlight search and live 'widgets'. The Spotlight search allows you to quickly find a contact, an app, an email, a message, calendar event, an app store listing or a Wikipedia page. The Today screen also shows: the date and time, Reminders and Calendar appointments, weather, news from Apple News (see page 213), Maps Destinations, such as how long it'll take to get home (see page 141), and suggestions from the Photos app (see page 176).

(see page 213)

(see page 141)

(see page 176)

Above: The Today screen offers a snapshot of information.

BASIC iPHONE NAVIGATION

It's time to learn a few of the basic touch-screen gestures. The lack of a Home button on newer iPhones has changed this significantly. Where necessary we'll explain how the methods differ.

- **Opening Apps**: Simply touching an app icon will open that app, full screen, on your iPhone.

- **Going Home**: Pressing the Home button will take you back to the Home screen. On iPhones without a Home button swipe up from the very bottom of the screen.

- **Summon Siri**: Bring up the iPhone's personal assistant by holding down the Home button. If you don't have a Home button, hold down the power button or say 'Hey Siri'.

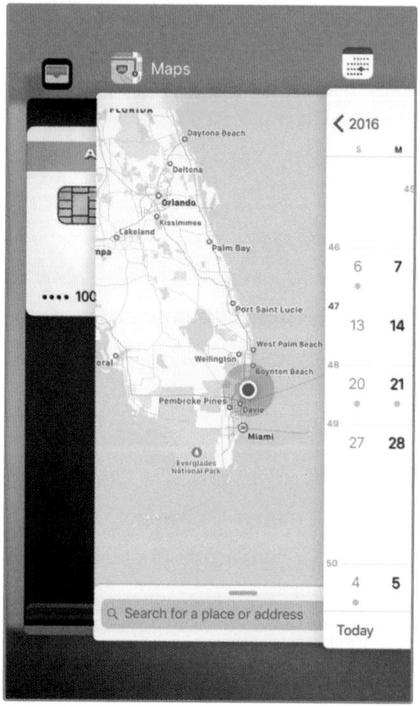

Multitasking

You can move between apps without returning to the Home screen. On phones with a Home button double click it when the screen is unlocked. For iPhones without a Home button, this is done via gestures – swipe up from the bottom of the screen, hold the app in place for a second, and release when other cards appear. Swipe left and right between open app cards and tap an app to re-open it.

Above: The multitasking screen makes it easy to swipe between open apps without returning to the Home screen.

Swiping and Scrolling

Moving your finger across the page to move to the next screen is a key means of navigating your way around the iPhone and will become second nature. Similarly, if you're reading a web page, email, etc. use a finger to move the screen around. The faster the flick, the faster the page moves.

Zooming

To zoom in on the iPhone place your thumb and forefinger on the screen and move them both away from each other. To zoom out, place your thumb and forefinger on the screen and move them towards each other in a pinching motion.

Screenshots

You might want to capture what's on your screen and save it as a photo. Press the power button and Home button together, or the power button and volume up button together.

3D Touch

A feature added to all phones since 2015, a firm press on the screen can be used to launch shortcuts from app icons, view messages, peek at content from other apps and much more. For example, you can press firmly on the Maps icon and select an option like Directions home, which saves time and effort.

Motion Sensors

The iPhone has a built-in sensor that knows when you switch the view from portrait to landscape – essentially turning the handset on its side.

Hot Tip

On larger iPhones it can be hard to reach apps at the top of the screen. Enable Reachability in Settings > Accessibility, then drag down on the bottom of the screen to bring these apps within reach.

Left and Above: Videos can be viewed in portrait (left) and landscape (above).

Above and Right: Turning the phone to landscape increases the size of the keyboard.

The iPhone Keyboard

The iPhone's virtual keyboard has a QWERTY layout. Here are the other basic keyboard buttons:

- **Shift**: Press the upward arrow once to type a single capital letter. Hit it twice in quick succession to enable Caps Lock.

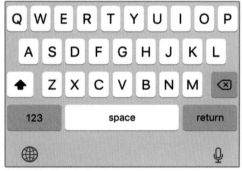

- **123**: This button switches the keyboard from letters to numbers and symbols.

- **Globe**: Switch to emoji or to other keyboards you may have installed.

- **Microphone**: Dictate the message to your iPhone, rather than typing it.

Above: The iPhone keyboard.

- **Space**: Move from one word to the next or double-tap for a full stop.

- **Delete**: Touching the cross deletes any entered text. Hold it down to delete at a faster rate.

Lock the Screen/iPhone

Pressing the power button once will turn off the screen and lock the phone; if you're playing music, this will not affect playback. It will also auto lock after a certain period of inactivity.

Waking the iPhone

If you've locked the screen or it has timed out due to inactivity you'll need to unlock it. This can be done via Touch ID, Face ID or the Passcode you entered during set up. Once unlocked the iPhone will then return to the screen you were viewing when the device was locked.

- **Touch ID**: The change in the Home button means you can press once. On older handsets you'll need to wake the screen first and then rest the registered finger on the reader.

- **Face ID**: On newer iPhones all you need to do is position the phone so it can see your face, look at it and wait a second for the animated padlock to switch to unlocked. Then swipe up from the bottom of the screen.

- **Passcode**: Sometimes it makes more sense to use the passcode. Tap in your passcode to unlock the phone.

iPhone Lock Screen

- **Media Control Panel**: When playing music, click the Home or power button to summon media controls.

- **Siri**: Hold down the Home or power button to talk to Siri.

- **Camera and Torch**: Long press the buttons on the bottom of the screen to launch these apps.

- **Alerts**: If you receive a notification, simply swipe it to go straight to it, after unlocking your phone.

- **Control/Notification Centers**: Swipe up or down from the top or bottom of the screen to access these.

- **Today Screen**: Swipe from left to right to access this.

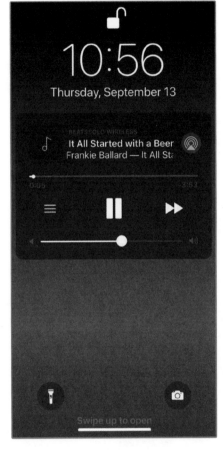

Above: Media controls, the camera app and Siri can still be used from the iPhones lock screen.

Shut Down

To switch off the iPhone, hold down the power switch for around 2–3 seconds when the phone is unlocked. The screen will go dark aside from a swipe bar, which requires you to 'slide to power off'. On the iPhone X and newer, hold the power button down in combination with the volume down button.

BASIC iPHONE SETTINGS

Here are a few basic settings that you may wish to adjust while using your iPhone. Access some of these by tapping the grey Settings icon on the Home screen, and others in the Control Center.

Below: The Control Center offers quick access to key settings by swiping up (iOS 11 and earlier phones) or down (iOS 12).

CONTROL CENTER

The iOS Settings app is home to the nuts and bolts of the OS, but you can quickly adjust some settings from the Control Center. On iPhone X or later swipe down from the top right of the screen to bring up the menu. In iOS 11 and on earlier phones this is accessed by swiping up from the bottom.

- **Connectivity Menu:** Airplane Mode switches off all cellular and internet activity. You can also turn off Wi-Fi, cellular data and Bluetooth.

- **Portrait Orientation Lock:** This will prevent the phone switching to landscape when turned on its side.

- **Do Not Disturb:** Represented by the moon icon. DND settings can be adjusted in the main settings app.

- **Screen Brightness:** Slide the meter up or down to alter this setting.

- **Screen Mirroring:** Allows you to send media to AirPlay-enabled devices like Apple TV over Wi-Fi.

- **Torch**: Switch your device's flashlight on and off.

- **Timer**, **Calculator and Camera**: Tapping these icons takes you straight to these apps.

- **Music**: Quickly access playback controls and volume.

- **Screen Recording**: From iOS 11, you can record the content of your display.

- **Home**: Tap the House icon to quickly control your smart home devices.

- **Apple TV Remote**: If you have an Apple TV in your home set up, you can tap this icon to load a mini remote control interface.

NIGHT SHIFT

Night Shift enables you to lower the colour temperature of the display to limit exposure to sleep-affecting blue light. In Display & Brightness > Night Shift, you can set a schedule, manually enable and alter the temperature.

WALLPAPER

By selecting Settings > Wallpaper you can also alter the appearance of your phone. On the left is the lock screen wallpaper and on the right is the Home screen wallpaper. Select Choose a New Wallpaper to change them to a new wallpaper or to a photo from your Camera Roll. Once you've chosen the new picture, press Set.

Hot Tip

While optimal screen brightness is preferable, it also has a negative effect on battery life, which can be preserved by turning the brightness down.

Below: iOS offers Dynamic wallpapers, which look like they move, but these cause greater drain on battery life.

SOUNDS

You can tinker with the sounds emanating from your phone when calls or notifications arrive.

Changing Ringtones and App Alerts

Enter Settings > Sounds to control volume and vibration, and to customize sounds for each volume type. The Sounds and Vibration Patterns menu allows you to control the precise sound and vibration style for each type of notification. For example, press Text Tone to bring up all of the available options. Selecting one of the options will place a tick next to the name and play a preview. Once you're happy with your choice, press the Back button and your selection will be saved.

Below: You can increase the security of your iPhone by choosing a passcode. You can enter the passcode each time you unlock your phone, or use Touch ID/Face ID.

Controlling Ringer Volume

To adjust your ringtone volume, simply drag the onscreen slider left or right within the Settings > Sounds menu. It's also easy to control the ringtone volume by pressing the physical volume keys on the side of the device when on the Home screen. This will bring up an onscreen indicator showing the volume meter increasing or decreasing.

SECURITY

Losing a smartphone can be more dangerous than losing your credit cards, bank details and address book in one fell swoop. Here's how to protect your data.

Face ID, Touch ID and Passcode

Security methods prevent unwanted guests accessing your iPhone beyond the lock screen. If you skipped this step on setup, enter Settings and select General. Scroll down to Face ID/Touch ID (depending on your model) and Passcode. Here you'll be able to set-up biometric information and choose which apps can make use of them. If you have an iPhone with a Touch ID sensor, you can add additional digits here. This is also where you change your change your passcode.

Auto-Lock

Within Settings > Display & Brightness you can configure the period of inactivity necessary for the phone to lock itself. The default is 30 seconds, but you can choose from between Never and 5 minutes.

SYNCING CONTENT ON YOUR iPHONE

There are a number of ways to ensure that the information you carry around with you on your iPhone is up to date. You can sync information using iTunes and iCloud; both have their merits and we'd advise you make use of both.

Syncing via iTunes with USB

The traditional way to sync content on an iPhone is to plug it into your computer via the bundled-in USB cable. Once you plug the device in, the iTunes program should launch. You'll see your iPhone appear as a button in the navigation bar in iTunes. Click the iPhone icon and select the Sync option at the bottom of the Summary tab.

Syncing via iTunes over Wi-Fi

You can sync content over Wi-Fi when your computer and iPhone are on the same Wi-Fi network. Here's how to set it up:

1. Plug the iPhone into your computer; iTunes will launch. Select your iPhone from the top navigation menu. In the Summary tab, scroll down to the Options section.

Hot Tip

Selecting 'Never' from the Auto-Lock settings screen will mean your screen stays on unless you manually hit the power button. This will drain your battery life fast.

Below: To keep your iPhone up to date, you can use iCloud or sync it to iTunes using Wi-Fi or a USB cable.

2. Tick the box that says 'Sync with this iPhone over Wi-Fi' and press Sync to save the changes.

3. iTunes syncing will now take place when your iPhone and computer are on the same network.

What is Synced via iTunes?

iTunes syncs all of the applications, including: music, TV shows, movies, web bookmarks, books, contacts, calendars, notes, documents and ringtones you have downloaded. iTunes will also download new content that you've acquired via your phone and vice versa.

Syncing Your iPhone via iCloud

If you agreed to use iCloud when setting up the device, it will automatically sync information from some of the iPhone's most important applications, plus others you've downloaded along with all media purchases, making that information seamlessly available at iCloud.com and across any other Apple devices you may have.

What is Synced via iCloud?

Enter Settings > Your Name > iCloud to choose what information you'd like to sync to your iCloud account. Among the options are: Contacts, Calendars, Reminders, Safari, Notes and more. Turning these on in the iCloud settings will mean any changes you make are saved via iCloud.

Hot Tip

Syncing information via iCloud will not back up all information. If you delete a contact on your iPhone, it will be deleted from iCloud too.

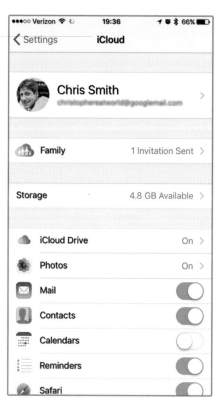

Above: You can choose which aspects of your iPhone you wish to sync via iCloud.

BACKING UP YOUR iPHONE

A backup will restore important information if you need to perform a full reset or if you wish to pick up where you left off on a new device. You can back up via iTunes or iCloud but not both.

Backing Up via iCloud

Apple gives you 5 GB of free storage to store important data. If you choose to enable backups, press Settings > Your Name > iCloud. Scroll down to Backup and toggle the switch to 'on'. If enabled, iCloud backups are automatically made when your phone is on a Wi-Fi network, plugged in and locked.

Buying More iCloud Storage Space

5GB of free space isn't a lot. If you want to store your photos and videos, you'll need to buy a storage plan from Settings > iCloud > Storage. They start at 79p/99¢ a month for 50GB.

Backing Up via iTunes

Backing up via iTunes safeguards everything on your phone, including your photos, to a computer allowing you to restore it all in the event of loss or failure. Plug your phone into your computer and iTunes should load.

Above: Backing up using iCloud.

1. Select the iPhone in the iTunes menu. From the Backup menu, tick the box that says Back up to this computer.

2. Select Apply to save the changes, and then press Sync to back up the phone.

What Information is Backed Up?

Backups over iCloud and iTunes will safeguard all photos on your Camera Roll, all of your account settings (email, Facebook, Twitter, etc.), documents, general phone settings, Contacts, Calendar and more, and make it easy to pick up where you left off if you restore from a backup.

iTunes vs iCloud: Which Should I Use?

As there are two options for backing up your data, it's sometimes difficult to pick the best one for you. Both options have their advantages; the following guide should help you decide.

- **iTunes**: If you prefer to have information saved on your computer rather than on the internet, choose iTunes. This can be the better option for restoring absolutely everything on your phone. Restoring an iPhone via USB connection is also faster than via iCloud.

- **iCloud**: To go truly wireless, you need to use iCloud. This will enable you to restore your device or set up a new phone with all of your information without connecting to a computer. Also, if you're not backing up that much data, Wi-Fi iCloud backups are quick and simple. However, to back up everything you'll probably need more than the free 5GB of storage.

iOS SOFTWARE UPDATE

Apple releases a new version of iOS every year. The latest version is iOS 12, which came out in September 2018. It's not just the new iPhone XS, XS Max and iPhone 8 that get iOS 12. If you own an iPhone 5S (released in 2013), you can also update and access the new features.

Updating Software

Once a new update is available, you'll receive a notification telling you it is ready to download. You'll also see a badge icon next to the Settings app. Go to Settings > General > Software Update to see what the update is. Here's how to download it:

Hot Tip

For everything about restoring from an iTunes or iCloud backup, see the Advanced iPhone chapter.

1. Back up your iPhone, in case something goes wrong. Ensure you're connected to Wi-Fi and your battery is at least half charged or connected to a power source.

2. Go to Settings > General > Software Update > Install Now.

3. The update should install (you'll see the progress meter).

4. Once finished it will restart and you'll have the latest software.

NOTIFICATIONS

The well-connected iPhone user is constantly receiving emails, messages, social networking updates, upcoming Calendar events, Reminders, app updates, missed phone calls and more.

NOTIFICATION CENTER

You'll see new notifications on your lock screen. However, to see the Notification Center place your finger anywhere on the lock screen and swipe up. You'll see notifications from all of your apps from 'earlier today' and 'yesterday'. It could be a Skype message, a Facebook message, news alert or anything in between. Tapping a notification opens the app, swiping from right to left presents options to Manage, View or Clear.

Grouped Notifications

In iOS 12 lock screen notifications from the same app are grouped together in a stack. So, instead of seeing seven notifications from Messages and four from Mail, you'll see them together. Tapping the stack expands the notifications so you can see them individually.

Notification Previews

Notification previews give you an idea of what a message entails, but leave them open to prying eyes. Go to Settings > Notifications and select an app. Scroll to Show Previews and choose from Always, When Unlocked or Never.

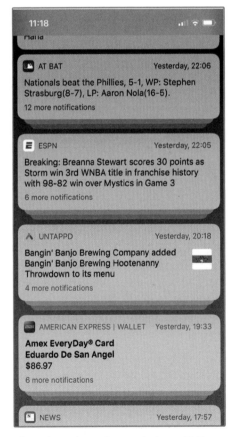

Above: The Notification Center stacks alerts in iOS 12.

ALERT STYLE

Within the Settings > Notifications menu you can also configure the type of alert you'll receive. Select an app from the list to see the options.

- **Allow Notifications**: If you don't want to be alerted by this app then turn off the Allow Notification toggle switch.

- **Alerts**: Choose the style of the alert, by ticking the respective boxes. You can choose if an alert comes to the lock screen, sits in the Notification Center or presents a Banner notification at the top of the screen, while the phone is unlocked. You can choose from Temporary Banners, which disappear quickly, or Persistent, which force you to respond or dismiss them.

- **Sounds**: You can also toggle sounds on and off on this screen.

- **Badges**: Some app settings enable the option to add show badges – a red dot next to the app icon when you have an alert. The dot also features the number of unread alerts.

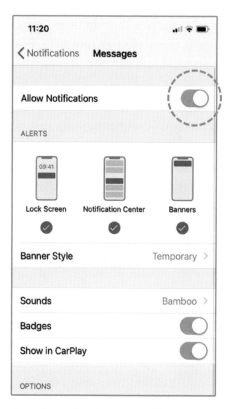

Above: You can choose how you would like an alert to appear on your screen.

Quiet Notifications

In iOS 12 there is an option to Deliver Quietly, which means notifications will arrive in the Notifications Center, without appearing anywhere else. From the Notifications Center, gently swipe from right to left on a notification and select Manage. Here you can select Deliver Quietly, or Turn Off completely. You can also hit Settings to fine tune the notification settings for that app.

ORGANIZING

Have we already mentioned that the iPhone is multi-talented? The device features a host of built-in apps to ensure you never sleep in, never burn dinner and always remember that Eureka idea.

CALENDAR

The iPhone's built-in Calendar app will sync all appointments from your email and social networking accounts, while new events can be segregated into Work, School and Home sections. Apple's online storage iCloud platform ensures that any new appointments you add using your iPhone will appear across your other Apple devices.

Below: You can add specific events to your iPhone calendar and request multiple reminders.

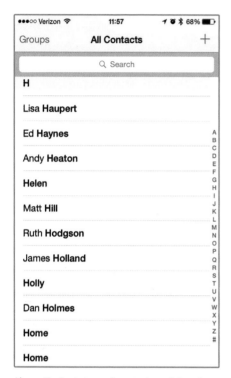

Above: The Contacts app allows you to scroll through your address book and select people to message or call.

ADDRESS BOOK

Your phone contacts should naturally be imported on to the device when you first insert the SIM card, but it's best to check with your network, as in some cases, you may have to back them up first. You can also import contacts from Microsoft Exchange, Facebook, Twitter, Google, iCloud and more. Learn how to manage your contacts in chapter two.

CALCULATOR

The built-in touch-screen calculator, which sits within the Utilities folder on your Home screen, makes it easy to split dinner bills, work out household budgets and even resolve complex formulas.

Hot Tip

Turn the iPhone on its side to switch to the scientific calculator.

CLOCK

As well as the clock that sits within the center of your title bar, there is a standalone Clock app on your Home screen, which includes a World Clock, Alarm, Stopwatch and Timer.

World Clock

The World Clock is a handy feature. By default, the iPhone features Cupertino (Apple's headquarters in California), New York and London, but you can add other locations to the list.

Left: World Clock lets you view the time across multiple locations.

Alarm Clock

Mobile phones have been consigning the trusty alarm clock to the scrapheap for years, and the iPhone continues that tradition.

1. Select the Clock app, and press the Alarm icon at the bottom of the screen and press the + icon in the top right to add a new alarm.

2. Use the scrollable wheels to set the hour, minute and AM/PM settings. Press the Repeat option to select which days you'd like the alarm to go off.

3. Select Sound to choose an alarm (choose from default ringtones, 'Pick a song' from your music library or select Tones Store to head to the iTunes store).

4. Toggle Snooze on or off to give you the option of an extra 10 minutes, and press Label to give the alarm a name, i.e. work, feed dog, etc. When you are satisfied, click Save to return to the Alarm screen. From there, you can toggle the alarm on or off.

5. Selecting the Edit button in the top-right corner enables you to delete the alarm completely or change the settings discussed above.

Stopwatch

Although now an afterthought on a smartphone, the stopwatch is still useful.

Above: Alarm Clock allows you to save multiple alarms with your choice of repeat, sound and snooze options.

Above: The timer screen gives you access to sound options as well as displaying cancel and pause buttons.

Timer

Set a countdown. Handy if you've got something in the oven.

1. Select Clock > Timer and use the vertical scroll wheels to set how many hours and how many minutes you'd like to count down from.

2. Choose an alert to sound when the timer runs out by selecting 'When Timer Ends' and choosing from available ringtones.

3. Press Start to begin the timer, and a new screen will launch, informing you of how long is left and also enabling you to pause or cancel the timer.

Bedtime

Introduced in iOS 10, Bedtime was designed to promote healthy sleep by going to bed and waking up at the same time. To set it up you'll answer a few questions about what time you want to get up, how much sleep you need and when you'd like a reminder it's bedtime, and you'll choose an alarm. You'll then be notified of your progress over time.

NOTES, REMINDERS AND VOICE MEMOS

The iPhone features a number of ways for you to preserve information you're liable to forget. Here are three apps that specialize in remembering, so you don't have to.

Notes

The Notes app is given its own icon on the Home screen. All of your previous notes will be listed, accessible and editable with one touch. You can also select the on screen 'New' button to start a new note and use the keyboard to begin typing away. All notes will be automatically stored without having to save them. From iOS 10 you can add photos, handwritten scribbles and more to Notes.

Reminders

This excellent to do list application allows you to check off items, receive alerts for things you haven't done and create lists of reminders. Here's how to add a reminder:

1. Tap the + icon to add a new reminder or list. Select Reminder.

2. Enter your Reminder and select a date or time to be reminded. You can also choose to be reminded at a location, e.g., receive a reminder to send an email when you get to work.

3. Select the list you'd like to add it to and choose the priority of the reminder. When complete, select Done.

Hot Tip

To sync all of your notes to iCloud, hit Settings > iCloud and toggle the Notes switch to on. You can also change the font by entering Settings > Notes.

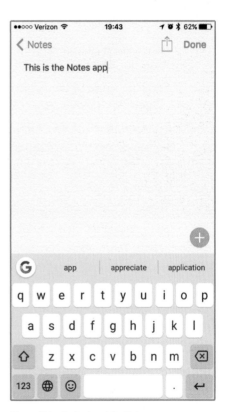

Above: Using the keyboard, the Notes app allows you to store thoughts, ideas and lists.

4. The item will then show up within the chosen list and within the Scheduled tab.

5. You'll receive notifications at the time/location. They'll also appear on the Today screen. Open the notification or go back into the app to tap the circle and mark it as complete.

Setting Reminders in Other Apps

Reminders works with many other iPhone features. You can ask Siri to set you a Reminder or, when receiving a phone call you can't answer, you can tap 'Remind Me' to ensure you return the call. It also works in apps like Safari and Maps; just press the Share button and select reminders.

Adding To Do Lists

Reminders could be for work, school or grocery shopping. So the Reminders app enables you to segregate them into lists. To add a list, tap the + in the top right of the main app and select Add List.

Sharing To Do Lists

Thanks to iCloud, you can work collaboratively on to do lists, which is great if you're planning a holiday, for example. If you select a list you can tap Edit > Sharing > Add Person to allow someone else to access the list.

> ### Hot Tip
> **If iCloud Family Sharing is enabled, the Family list is automatically shared with your linked family.**

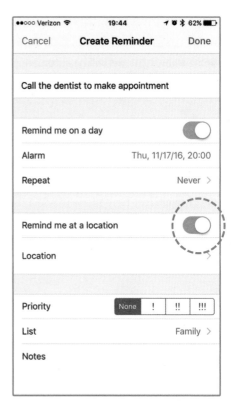

Above: You can choose to receive reminders when at a particular location.

Voice Memos

The Voice Memos app allows you to record conversations, random great ideas, interviews, humorous anecdotes, messages for friends and family, and more.

1. Launch the Voice Memos app from within the Utilities folder on the Home screen. Select the red record button to begin recording.

2. The time counter and wave form indicator will begin as soon as you press the button, and indicate that you are recording.

3. The waveform indicator will monitor the volume of the sound being recorded, which can help if you're recording interviews for example.

4. Once you've finished recording, press the Done button to the right. You can name the recording by tapping the default name.

5. All recordings can be accessed beneath the recording interface. In iOS 12 you'll need to tap the three dots to edit, duplicate or share the recordings.

Above: The VU indicator in the Voice Memos app allows you to keep track of recording volume.

Hot Tip

You can exit the Voice Memo app while recording and use other phone functions without interrupting the recording. Just tap the red indicator on the title bar to return to the app.

MAKING CALLS

Basic calling is simple: tap a name in your Contacts, tell Siri to 'call Chris', or touch a name to return a recent call – but there's much more. The iPhone also supports video and conference calls, and this section will show you how.

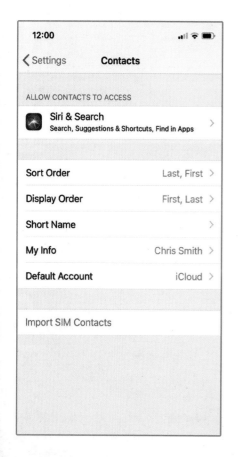

CONTACTS

Setting up your contacts in a smart way is crucial for making your iPhone work harder for you and minimising the ease with which you can find the numbers you need. Once your contacts are imported, you'll find phone numbers, email addresses, and Facebook info for everyone in your address book. Tap the Phone app, press the Contacts icon and dive in.

Importing Contacts

How you add your old contacts on to your new iPhone will depend on where they are stored. The most common ways to achieve this are the following:

○ **From a SIM card:** Insert the SIM card containing all your contacts into your new iPhone (you'll need to choose another option if the SIM cards of your old and new phones are not the same size). Go to Settings > Contacts > Import SIM Contacts.

Left: You can import contacts from a SIM card. This is the best way to transfer such information across from your old phone to your new iPhone.

- **Switching from Google Android**: As we explained during set-up (*see* page 27), there's a great Move to iOS app which will accomplish this for you, provided you still have your old iPhone.

- **From iCloud**: If you're upgrading from an old iPhone, all of your contacts should already be stowed in iCloud and will appear on the phone when you set up.

- **From iTunes**: If you've backed up an old iPhone via iTunes (*see* page 43), you will be able to restore your contacts from that backup. This is also ideal if your old phone is lost or broken.

- **From a Microsoft Exchange ActiveSync**: If you use your iPhone to pick up work email, then contacts can also be synced during set-up. For details on setting up Exchange, *see* page 117.

Merging Duplicate Contacts

You can merge duplicate contacts, from SIM and iCloud, into one entry in your Contacts app. Open the contact in question, click Edit in the top-right corner of the page for that entry and then scroll down to the bottom to find the Link Contact button. Tap this and select the contact(s) you wish to link.

Adding Contacts Manually

There are two main methods for adding new people into your Contacts:

Right: You can transfer your contacts from a Google Android phone by using the Move to iOS app that can be downloaded from the Google Play Store.

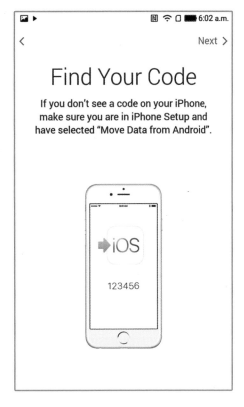

6:02 a.m.

<   Next >

Find Your Code

If you don't see a code on your iPhone, make sure you are in iPhone Setup and have selected "Move Data from Android".

➡iOS

123456

- **Brand new contact**: From within Contacts, tap the + button. This will bring up a form for you to fill in with the person's details, such as First Name, Last Name, Phone Number, Email, Address as well as their birthday and anniversary dates. From here, you can also assign things such as ringtone, text tone and photo, or apply social networking preferences.

- **Previous caller**: Open your Recent Call list and scroll to the number you wish to add. Tap on the blue arrow next to it and then select 'Create New Contact'. You can then enter the relevant information for them.

Below: While connected to Wi-Fi, you can sync your contacts using iCloud by selecting 'iCloud' from the 'Settings' menu.

SYNCING CONTACTS

Once you have imported your contacts on to your iPhone, you need to ensure they're kept safe and up to date. It's now easier than ever to back up and synchronize vital information, and to make it readily available to access wherever you are and across all your devices – computer, iPad or other iPhone. The best way to do this is wirelessly through Apple's iCloud platform.

Syncing Contacts Using iCloud

If you already set up iCloud (see page 29), then your contacts should automatically be synced. If not, you'll need to be connected to Wi-Fi before you follow these steps:

1. Tap Settings on your Home screen and tap your name to access your profile.

2. Enter iCloud settings, tap Account and, if you haven't already done so while setting up, add

in your Apple ID and password. From here, you can choose which of the services you'd like to sync using the On/Off switches. In this instance, you just need to ensure you've turned on Contacts.

Syncing Contacts Using iTunes

We wouldn't recommend this, but if you prefer to manage your information on a larger screen, then connecting to iTunes via a USB cable is your best bet, but first you'll have to turn off over-the-air syncing on iCloud otherwise you'll end up with duplicates.

1. Go to Settings > Mail, Contacts, Calendars, select iCloud and switch off Contacts.

2. Connect the iPhone to your computer and iTunes should launch automatically. If it is on the same Wi-Fi network, it should sync automatically (see page 41).

Searching Contacts

Using the iPhone's touch screen to scroll rapidly up and down through your Contacts list is probably the most intuitive way to find that person you want to call or email, but there are other shortcuts.

○ **Jump to contacts by letter**: Use the alphabet on the right to quickly view all the names on your list.

○ **Simple search**: Start typing the name of the

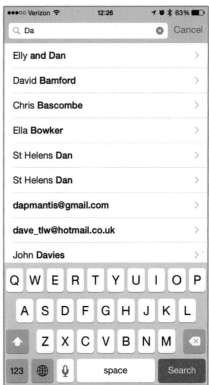

Above: You can search your contacts by typing the name you are looking for into the search bar at the top of the screen. This will quickly filter through your contact list.

contact you're hunting for into the search bar at the top of the screen. Your contacts will automatically filter to display matches.

Organizing Your Contacts Using Groups

Depending on which accounts you have added to your iPhone, contacts will be split into various Groups in your contact book. For example iCloud, Google and Twitter all get their own Groups. However, you can filter which Groups appear in your overall contacts listing – and here's how:

1. Enter Contacts and select Groups. At first, you're likely to see all Groups listed with a tick mark.

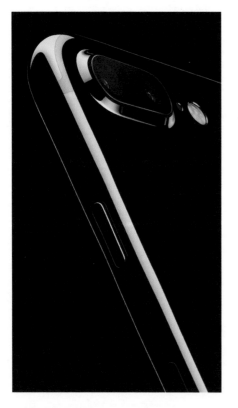

2. To turn off certain Groups (such as Gmail), you can tap a Group to remove the tick mark.

3. Tap Done and all the contacts within the Groups you selected will not show up.

Editing and Deleting Contacts

To change contact information or delete someone who is now out of your good books, go to Contacts and select the entry you want to amend or remove. Once the contact is open, click Edit and you can freely add, amend and delete details using the green + buttons or the red circles. If you want to delete the contact entirely then scroll to the bottom and hit Delete Contact.

Sharing Contacts

'Can you send me their number?' is a question that gets most people scrabbling through their phonebook, before reading out the answer while someone else taps it into their phone;

however, there is a faster way to share contacts. Simply tap the contact you wish to send, tap Share Contact and you can send the info by email, text message or AirDrop (see page 222).

SETTING UP YOUR 'MY INFO' CARD

The information on your 'My Info' card gets shared whenever you send someone your contact details. In order to edit this information, go to Contacts. Your card will be right at the top. Select it and tap Edit. From here, you can add your address, birthday, website, next of kin, social media profiles and more.

FAVOURITES

Your Favourites are the contacts you interact with the most. Just like speed dial on a normal phone, you can store all the vital numbers you'll be using. These favourites appear in the Phone app in a dedicated tab at the bottom of the screen.

Adding Favourites

It'd be amazing if the iPhone could automatically fill up your Favourites group based on the number of times you've interacted with people in your phonebook but, currently, anointing a Favourite is still your choice. Plus, it might be embarrassing to have that takeaway listed at No. 1. You can add multiple favourites (e.g. different phone numbers, or message) for a single contact. There are two methods for adding a new Favourite:

Below: Setting up a My Info card makes it easier to share all of your information in one fell swoop.

- **When you're viewing a contact**: Select the Add to Favourites button.

- **From within your Favourites**: Tap the + symbol in the top-right corner and select which method of contact you'd like to add to favourites (i.e. call mobile, send an email etc.)

Add Favourites Widget to the Today Screen

The Today screen (swipe left) can be customised to feature widgets from practically any app you want. It should feature Favourite contacts by default, offering quick access. However, if not, simply scroll to the bottom of Today, hit Edit and find 'Favourites' from More Widgets. You can then hit Edit again to move it up the list so it appears closer to the top of the Today page.

Calling a Favourite

It's simple. Select the Phone app icon and then select Favourites from the bottom-left corner of the screen. Pick the person you want to call, tap their name and you're dialling.

DIALLING

Time to make a call! Start by selecting the Phone icon on the Home screen and this will bring up the familiar number keypad, plus four other options along the bottom: Favourites, Recents, Contacts and Voicemail. You can then choose how you want to dial.

Above: It's easy to add a contact to your Favourites.

- **Know the number?** Use the keypad to enter the digits, then press the green call button.

12:30

Hey Siri call my wife
Tap to Edit

Calling Meaghan – mobile:

Above: It's easy to make calls with Siri without searching through the iPhone to find the contact.

- **Dialling a recently dialled number or missed call**: Tapping the Recents icon opens your call log, showing all the incoming, outgoing and missed calls. Touch the blue 'i' button to see more details of who called or tap the name to return the call.

- **Dialling using Favourites**: Press the Favourites icon to call up all your personal VIPs and touch anywhere on their name to start dialling.

- **Calling from Contacts**: Select Contacts from the bottom of the screen. Scan your address book by scrolling, searching or using the A–Z strip and then tap on the contact you wish to call to bring up their Contact card.

Voice Dialling

It's easy to make a call using only your voice. Apple's take on voice control – the personal assistant Siri – is leading the way. If you have Siri activated (Go to Settings > General > Siri), just fire up Siri in your preferred way, then say 'Call Bob'. Siri will launch the Phone app and dial for you.

HANDS-FREE

In the previous section, we showed you how to use voice dialling with Siri to make a call. If you want to make the entire conversation a hands-free affair so you can apply your opposable thumbs to more important things, such as taking dinner out of the oven before it burns, here's how you can do that with your iPhone:

- **Put your phone on speakerphone**: From the Call screen, you'll see a Speaker icon. Tap this at any time during the call and the audio will play back through the iPhone's built-in speaker. Tap the icon again to turn off speakerphone and return to your phone's normal speaker.

- **Use a wired headset**: You can use the Apple EarPods that come boxed with your phone or you can buy a pair from another manufacturer. There are hundreds to choose from, but make sure you get a pair with a built-in microphone and a center button you can press to answer calls.

- **Use a Bluetooth headset**: You can skip the cables entirely and pair your phone with a wireless Bluetooth headset. After you've paired it once, any time you're in range of your iPhone (and your iPhone's Bluetooth is switched on), your headset will automatically connect, leaving you free to answer and make calls without ever touching your phone.

Above: Call screen with the Bluetooth headset option selected.

- **Connect the car**: Most new cars come with a Bluetooth-enabled media system. Make sure your iPhone Bluetooth is switched on and then follow the pairing instructions on your car media system. Once paired, many car systems offer enhanced controls such as phonebook syncing and calls controlled via buttons on the steering wheel.

○ **Use CarPlay**: If you've bought a brand new car in the last couple of years, chances are Apple's CarPlay is on board. This effectively puts your iPhone homescreen on your car's infotainment display.

How to Pair a Bluetooth Device with Your iPhone

1. Make sure the device you're connecting with your iPhone is discoverable.

2. On your iPhone, go to Settings > Bluetooth and switch on Bluetooth.

3. The iPhone will scan for available devices with which to pair and you should see your device listed. The name displayed will depend on what the manufacturer allocated, but hopefully it should be obvious. Select your device and, if prompted, enter the pairing code allocated by the manufacturer (see the product manual).

Hands-free Siri

In addition to making hands-free calls with Siri's voice dialling, it's also possible to use Siri to start calls, without having to touch your iPhone. You can also write and send messages, schedule meetings, get directions, set reminders and search the web, simply by talking. Siri works with

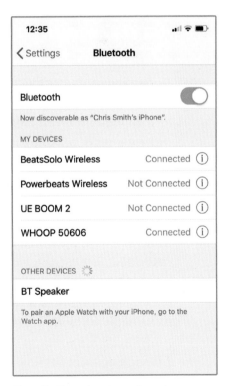

Hot Tip

If you're prompted for a code while pairing Bluetooth devices, try entering '0000'. This is often the default code used by device manufacturers.

Above: The Bluetooth settings can be used to pair other Bluetooth devices with your phone.

the headphones that came with your iPhone or you can buy your own compatible wired or Bluetooth headset, or just use the built-in speaker.

- ○ **To start talking to Siri**: You can speak to Siri without touching your phone, just say 'Hey Siri' near your phone. As long as 'Allow "Hey Siri"' is on (Settings > Siri) Siri will come to life and ask what you'd like to do. You can then fire off instructions, such as 'Call Dave'.

- ○ **To continue a conversation with Siri**: Once you've got Siri's attention, you can ask anything. In some cases you'll be asked questions you can continue the conversation by asking, but in others you'll need to say 'Hey Siri' again.

- ○ **Sending hands-free messages**: You can dictate messages and emails via your headset mic to Siri. She'll show you a preview and ask if you're ready to send. Answer 'yes' or 'no' or tap the screen to confirm.

CONFERENCE CALLS

A conference call allows groups of people to connect on a single phone call. They are mainly used for business meetings, but they also provide a great way for families to catch up over long distances. Provided your mobile phone network allows it, you can create iPhone conference calls. Alternatively, for international calls, you can use services such as Skype and FaceTime over the internet.

Managing a Conference Call

Conference calls are often prearranged with a designated list of attendees and one person taking responsibility for

Above: You can dictate messages to Siri and send them without touching the phone.

'chairing' the conference. However, the iPhone makes it very easy to bring people into existing calls, here's how you turn a one-to-one call into a conference.

- **Make your first call**: For a prearranged conference call, you'll need to dial one of the people joining the call first in the usual way (see page 62 for help with dialling).

- **To add a second person**: While on your first call, tap Add Call and then make another call. Next, select Merge Calls. Repeat as necessary to add up to five people to the discussion.

- **To remove an attendee from the call**: People can obviously leave of their own free will, but should you need to eject someone, select the 'i' icon on the call screen and tap End next to the person's name.

- **To chat privately with one person during the call**: To have a bit of secret sideline whispering with someone on the call, just tap 'i' and then press Private next to the person you want to speak to. Hit Merge Calls when you're ready to resume the conference.

- **Adding an incoming caller**: If an incoming caller wishes to join the call, simply tap Hold Call + Answer, then tap Merge Calls and this person will be added to your conference call.

Right: Selecting 'Add Call' allows you to merge others into an existing call.

(see page 62 for help with dialling)

<figure>
Hot Tip

The more Siri knows, the better. Create Contact cards with nicknames, addresses and email addresses to help Siri respond better to your requests. To add a nickname, find a contact, select Edit > Add Field > Nickname.
</figure>

RECEIVING CALLS

Taking incoming calls on the iPhone can be as easy as a single tap, but with a little customization, you can tailor your phone to respond to calls in a way that suits you best, based on who's calling, where you are or what you're doing at the time.

ACCEPTING CALLS

Life is full of decisions, and each time your iPhone lights up, rings or buzzes with an incoming call, you've been handed another one to make. Ultimately, what you do next rests entirely on whether you're in the mood for talking, you're too busy for chit-chat or you just want to be left alone.

- **Answering a call**: If your phone is already unlocked, just tap the green icon to answer. If the phone is locked, drag the slider to answer or, if you have one, you can press the Home button to answer.

- **Calls from other Apps**: Apple now allows other apps to access the main calling interface. So, if you're getting a call from WhatsApp or Facebook Messenger it'll look like a regular call.

Right: When you receive an incoming call, you have the option to tap answer or tap Message or Remind Me if you don't wish to answer the call.

Rejecting Calls

We're here to help, not to judge, so whatever your reason is for rejecting a caller, here are the most straightforward ways to decline an inbound call:

○ **Decline a call and send it to voicemail**: Press the power button twice quickly.

○ **Silence a call**: To ignore a call without rejecting it, press the Power button once, flick the mute switch or press either volume button. You can still answer the call after silencing it, as long as you catch it before it goes to voicemail.

○ **Reply to an incoming call with a text message**: When the call comes in, tap the Message option and then choose a reply or tap Custom to send a carefully crafted brushoff of your own (to create your own default replies, go to Settings > Phone > Reply with Text and replace any of the default messages).

Right: Tap Message if you don't want to answer the call, but would like to acknowledge the caller with a text.

Meaghan Smith
WhatsApp Audio declined

Respond with:

Sorry, I can't talk right now.

I'm on my way.

Can I call you later?

Custom...

Cancel

Hot Tip

Make friends with the mute button on your iPhone and use it when you're not speaking so you'll be able to cut out background noise. It also leaves you free to sneeze, cough or have a conversation in the real world without anyone knowing.

- **Remind Me Later:** A handy feature that lets you reject a call but gives you a nudge in the ribs to call back when it's more convenient. When a call comes in, tap Remind to choose from 1 hour or When I leave.

Block Callers

You can block callers from the Recents tab in the phone app (see page 74). Tap the 'i' icon next to the name or number, scroll to the bottom of the screen and select Block this Caller.

Do Not Disturb Mode

Do Not Disturb was designed to prevent unwanted interruptions. Of course, cutting yourself off from the world entirely would mean emergency calls or special loved ones wouldn't get through, but Apple has thought of that. Do Not Disturb can be customized to enable exceptions. In iOS 12 you'll see a new lock screen notification telling you Do Not Disturb is enabled. Here's how to activate and fine-tune your built-in call buffer:

- **To quickly switch on Do Not Disturb:** To quickly switch on Do Not Disturb: Summon the Control Center (see page 38) and tap the moon icon. This manually enables Do Not Disturb. In iOS 12, use a longer 3D Touch press to configure for One Hour, Until This Evening or Until I Leave This Location.

Above: Use a 3D Touch press on the moon icon in Control Center to configure Do Not Disturb settings.

- **To schedule Do Not Disturb**: Go to Settings > Do Not Disturb and flick the on button to manually enable the setting. This will automatically silence calls and alerts. If you select Scheduled, you can configure it to turn on at regular times.

- **Bedtime**: In iOS 12, a new subset of Scheduled is Bedtime mode. Enable this to dim the lock screen, silence calls and keep notifications in the Notifications Center until the scheduled DND ends or until you unlock your phone in the morning.

- **To set exceptions**: Press the Allow Calls From button and choose from the following options: Favourites, Everyone, No One, All Contacts or a specific Group you've set up in your Contacts.

- **Repeated calls**: If you feel like making an exception that allows persistent callers through, you can fire up the Repeated Calls option. If this is switched on, anyone who calls you twice within three minutes will be able to disturb your slumber/meeting/prayers.

- **Do Not Disturb while driving**: From iOS 11, Apple automatically enabled Do Not Disturb while driving using GPS. You can alter this within Settings > Do Not Disturb and scroll down to Do Not Disturb While Driving.

Juggling Calls

The iPhone has various options that allow you to juggle multiple calls. Here they are:

- **Put current call on hold**: Touch and hold the Mute button. Press it again to resume.

Above: If you receive an incoming call while already on the phone, you will be presented with these options.

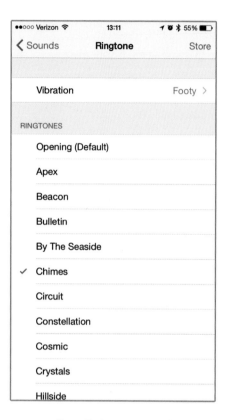

Above: The Ringtone setting screen allows you to preview and select which ringtone you would like. The selected tone will be highlighted with a tick next to it, as seen for 'Chimes', above.

Hot Tip

It's handy to change your ringtone from the default, if only so that you know it's your phone that's ringing when you're out.

- ⊙ **Put current call on hold while answering a new incoming call**: Tap the Hold + Accept button that appears when the second call comes in.

- ⊙ **Ignore call and send to voicemail**: Tap Decline.

- ⊙ **End the first call and answer the new one**: Press End + Accept.

- ⊙ **On a FaceTime video call**: You can either end the video call and answer the incoming call, or decline the incoming call.

- ⊙ **Switch between calls but keep both alive**: Tap Swap and the active call is put on hold.

If you're receiving a call from another iPhone user, you can tap FaceTime to switch to a FaceTime call.

RINGTONES

The iPhone comes with its own selection of chirpy ringtones, but the internet is full of thousands more and you can even make your own.

- ⊙ **Choosing a ringtone**: Go into Settings and choose Sounds > Ringtone. A scrollable list of available tones will appear. Tap any of the options for a preview; a tick will display next to the most recent tone you've listened to.

- **Buying and downloading new ringtones**: From your Home screen, select iTunes > More > Tones; here, you can trawl tones by categories and popularity. To purchase, click the Buy button and the ringtone will appear in your list.

- **Setting tones for calls, texts, emails and updates**: To edit which sounds are used for incoming texts, emails and app updates, head into Settings > Notifications; here you'll see the options to change the settings for all of your apps, including Messages and Phone.

- **Assigning ringtones to contacts**: Go into Contacts and select the person for whom you want to set a new ringtone. Hit Edit > Ringtone and choose from the list.

Feel the Vibrations

You can also customize the vibrating alerts you feel when you get a phone call. Regardless of your tone, you can choose a different vibration at Settings > Sounds & Haptics > Ringtone > Vibration. You can select from the options, or select 'Create New Vibration', which allows you to tap on the screen and create your own pattern. For example, you could assign this custom vibration to a particular contact so you know who is calling even if the phone is on silent.

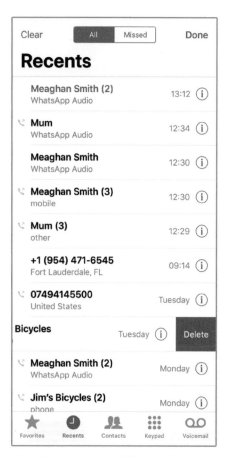

Above: Swiping an entry in the Calls list will display the Delete option in red. This entry can then be removed from your calling history.

RECENT CALLS SCREEN

The Recent Calls feature on the iPhone lets you review calls you've made, received or missed and is accessed via the Recents tab at the bottom of the Phone app. This list of calls can be filtered to display All (every incoming and outgoing call, whether answered or not) or Missed (incoming calls you didn't answer). You can also access details such as when the call was made, how long it lasted and contact information for the person you called or who tried to call you.

- **Call information**: Tap the small blue circle with the blue i icon to find out when a call was made, how long it lasted, when it started and finished, and any caller information stored in your Contacts.

- **To return a missed call**: Simply tap the name of the caller and the phone will dial.

- **To delete an entry from Recents**: Swipe any entry to the left and tap the red Delete button.

Hot Tip

If one of the calls listed is from someone who isn't in your phonebook, it's easy to add them. Just tap the blue 'i' icon, followed by Create New Contact and fill out their details. They will then show up in your Contacts.

VOICEMAIL

Voicemail is an essential tool for collecting messages while you're otherwise engaged. Some excellent new features on the iPhone now make it even easier to set up and manage this tool.

SETTING UP VOICEMAIL

The first time you tap Voicemail on your new iPhone, you will be prompted to create a password and to record a custom voicemail greeting. Getting set up should only take five minutes; here's how to get your voicemail up and running.

Recording a Personalized Greeting

The iPhone comes with a prerecorded generic voicemail greeting (which will vary, depending on your carrier). However, we recommend creating your own personal message. Before you begin recording, make sure that you're in a quiet place and that you've planned what you're going to say.

○ **To record your greeting**: Select Voicemail from the Phone app. If you have Visual Voicemail enabled (see overleaf), you'll see Greeting in the top left. Tap this and select Custom. You'll then be able to select Record.

Below: Greeting screen with the custom record a greeting option selected.

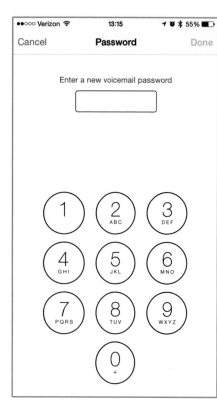

••○○○ Verizon 📶	13:15	✈ 🔋 ✳ 55% 🔋
Cancel	**Password**	Done

Enter a new voicemail password

1	2 ABC	3 DEF
4 GHI	5 JKL	6 MNO
7 PQRS	8 TUV	9 WXYZ
	0 +	

Above: You can select a password to protect your voicemail messages.

Hot Tip

Send an incoming call to voicemail by pressing the Power button twice. If you're using a headset, you can also tap the microphone twice to send the caller directly to voicemail.

○ **To review your greeting**: You can review the greeting by pressing Play. If you're happy, tap Save or, if you want another go, follow the steps above again.

○ **Visual Voicemail**: If Visual Voicemail isn't available on your mobile carrier, selecting Voicemail from the Phone app will call your voicemail. Listen to the audio instructions in order to record and save your greeting.

Set an Alert Sound for New Voicemail

You can assign a specific ringtone to alert you to new voice messages. Go to Settings > Sounds and tap New Voicemail, but remember that if the phone is set to silent, it won't sound alerts.

Change Your Voicemail Password

Your Voicemail is password-protected in case you lose your phone or have it stolen. To set yours up, go to Settings > Phone > Change Voicemail Password. This is also the password you'll use should you wish to dial in and collect your voicemail from another phone.

New Voicemail?

Firstly, you should receive a notification that appears on your lock screen; secondly, there'll be a red badge on the Phone app, and thirdly, you'll see another red badge next to the Voicemail icon within the Phone app. Some carriers will also send you a text message when you receive a voicemail.

VISUAL VOICEMAIL

Forget wasting time listening to voicemails in the order they were left! Visual Voicemail now lets you see all the messages in your Voicemail inbox and select which you listen to first. No more wading through 10-minute monologues from family members when you really need that vital work update. You may have to enable this manually, depending on your network.

Visual Voicemail Explained

Below is a list of the main things you need to pay attention to while you're using Visual Voicemail.

- **Caller info**: In most cases, the caller's name, phone number and location will appear, but where no details are available, you'll see Unknown or Private Caller.

- **The blue dot**: This signifies voicemails you've not yet listened to. If it doesn't have a blue dot, that message has already been played back.

Above: The Visual Voicemail screen allows you to prioritize which messages you want to listen to or delete first.

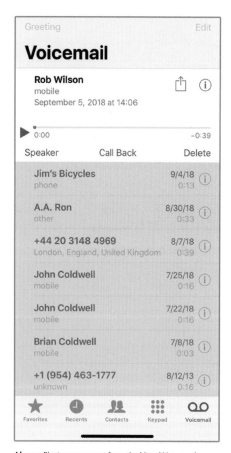

Above: Playing a message from the Visual Voicemail screen presents you with the options to Call Back or Delete.

Hot Tip

Your voicemail messages will be deleted in 30 days unless you save them.

○ **Playing a voicemail**: Tap the name or number of the message you'd like to hear, followed by the Play/Pause button.

○ **Access contact info**: Tap the blue 'i' icon that appears next to the caller's name and number. From here, you can also add this person to your Contacts.

○ **Fast-forward and rewind messages**: Drag the progress bar to jump to interesting points within a message, just like you would with an online video. Something from the message you need to hear again and write down? Just toggle back.

○ **Returning a call**: Press Call Back.

○ **Deleting a message**: Press Delete. If you do this by mistake scroll to the end and select Deleted Messages.

○ **Share:** Hit the Share button to send the voicemail to your email or forward it to another contact.

Retrieving Voicemail from Another Phone

If you don't have your phone with you, or the phone has run out of battery, you can still access your voicemails. Either dial your own phone number and follow the prompts (you'll need your voicemail password) or call your carrier's remote voicemail number. In both cases, you'll be back in a world where you have to listen to messages in sequence.

FACETIME

FaceTime is a great way to bring people together over long distances, letting you see fellow callers while you chat in real-time, or make calls over the internet.

Below: While on a FaceTime call, most of the screen will show the video image of the other caller, although there will be a smaller image of yourself shown at the bottom of your screen.

SETTING UP A FACETIME CALL

There are a multitude of ways to set up a FaceTime video or audio call. You can use the dedicated FaceTime app, you can begin a FaceTime call from a Contact card or you can take an existing phone call and convert it to a FaceTime call.

1. Enter the FaceTime app and select Video or Audio from the top menu. You can enter a Name, Email or Phone Number in the search field to begin the call, you can tap a recent FaceTime call from the list below, or press the + icon to choose from your contacts. Remember the recipient must be on iOS or Mac to receive the call.

2. Head to a contact card (from any app; it could be Contacts, Phone, Messages or Email) and, if that person is available to FaceTime, a video camera and phone receiver icon will be visible next to the FaceTime menu. Tap one to begin the call.

3. Dial the person you want to FaceTime as if you were making a normal call. Once the voice call is connected and you've decided to move to video, hit the FaceTime icon on the call screen. Once they've accepted, expect a short delay before their face appears on your display.

FaceTime Video calls

Once the FaceTime call is connected, in addition to the other person, you'll also see a smaller inset image of yourself on your phone screen. Three additional icons will also appear: Mute, End and Switch Cameras. The first two are self-explanatory; the latter lets you flick between the front and rear cameras – handy if you want to show someone something else in the room.

Above: When you receive an incoming call, you may wish to select the FaceTime option. If you do not wish outgoing calls to display this option, switch FaceTime off in settings.

FaceTime Audio Calls

These allow users to make audio-only calls via FaceTime. This is great because it allows users to make voice-over-internet (VoIP) calls without charging it to your mobile bill. It's perfect for calling internationally over Wi-Fi and mobile data and it's great if you're in an area with a poor mobile signal but abundant Wi-Fi, as it ensures better, clearer call quality.

Multitasking When Using FaceTime

A big bonus of iPhone's multitasking skills is the ability to use apps while on a FaceTime or a regular phonecall. It's great if you need to check diary dates, grab information from email, look something up on the internet or find something on a map. To do this, return to the Home screen while the FaceTime call is live and then navigate your phone as normal. When you decide to return to FaceTime or your call, simply tap the green bar at the top of the screen.

FaceTime Group Calls

A major new feature in iOS 12 enables iOS and macOS users to come together on a group FaceTime call. This is great if you want to gather people to a meeting, or just catch up with family members on a special occasion. Thirty-two people can feature on a FaceTime video/ audio call. In video the person speaking at the time will be front and center. When on a FaceTime call, simply tap the + button in the top-right corner to add contacts and repeat until everyone's on board. Then tap Audio or Video to begin the call.

Hot Tip

You can use FaceTime over your 4G network, but make sure you check your data plan first or you could end up with a hefty bill.

MESSAGING

Text and instant messaging remain the nation's most popular forms of communication. In this section we'll show you how to master the art of texting from your iPhone.

Below: The message screen allows you to send new messages, respond to messages and edit your message inbox.

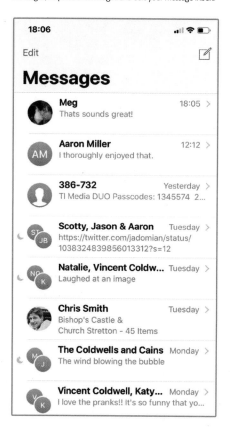

SENDING AN SMS

Sending text messages on the iPhone is painfree but there are many ways to acheive your desired effect:

- **To send a new message**: Tap the Messages icon on your Home screen to jump into the Messages app. Here, you'll see a list of all your received messages and a pencil and paper icon in the top-right corner. Press that icon and type in a contact number, start typing a name or hit the blue + button to choose someone from your address book.

Write your message in the field below and then hit Send. Your message will appear as a blue (or green for messages to non-iPhone users) bubble on the right of the conversation thread, and the word Delivered will appear underneath when it reaches its recipient. Replies will appear as white bubbles on the left of the thread.

- **Texting multiple people**: To send an SMS to more than one person – let's say to share a change of location for dinner – all you do is tap a second time in the To field and select a second contact from your address book. Repeat this for everyone you wish to contact.

- **To forward a text**: Hold down the bubbles containing the content you want to forward, select More from the pop-up and tap the Forward arrow, add a recipient and share away.

- **Failed texts**: When there's no network coverage sent messages will show as unsent messages in the conversation view. To try again, enter the conversation again, tap the red warning bubble and resend.

iMESSAGES

Apple's Messages app offers special functionality for messages between iOS and Mac users. iMessages are sent using Wi-Fi and so they can be sent to any iOS user around

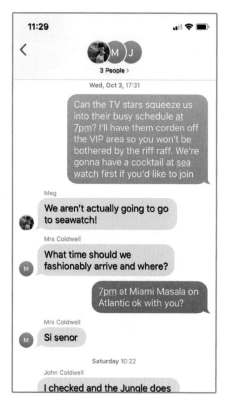

Above: You can start group chats with friends and family by putting more than one recipient in the 'To:' field.

the world without incurring charges. All of the features we're about to talk about can only be shared with other iPhone users.

Sending an iMessage

You send an iMessage in the same way as you would a regular text. If you're sending a message to someone with an iPhone, their name will appear in blue in the To field, and the message itself will show as a blue bubble when sent.

Hot Tip

iMessage not working? Head to Settings > Messages and ensure iMessage is toggled to 'on' at the top of the screen.

Receiving iMessages on Other Devices

Because iMessage is associated with your Apple ID, messages are received across all devices, which are signed in to that account. If you have an iPad or a Mac, iMessages can also be sent/received on those devices, with conversations synced.

RECEIVING SMS

Receiving and responding to incoming texts and iMessages will be one of the activities you do most with your new iPhone. In this section, we'll show you how to spot incoming messages.

Alerts and Notifications

In the Notifications section of the last chapter (*see* page 45) we told you how to customise the alerts you receive for each app and how to interact from

Left: Text message notifications also feature on the lock screen.

them. Depending on how you configure those settings, you'll receive messages on your lock screen, in your Notification Center and while you're using the phone. These can be signalled by a sound or a vibration as well as a visual alert.

○ **To respond to a message from a Banner notification**: Banner notifications appear at the top of the screen, and you can now drag down on the notification tab when it appears to bring up the keyboard interface, allowing you to reply easily. Or tap the banner to enter the messages app.

○ **To respond from a lock screen notification**: Whether it's on your lock screen or in the Notification Center, it's easy to interact with Message notifications. With a 3D Touch enabled phone long press on the alert to launch a mini message interface you can easily reply to. If the phone is locked, you'll need to use Face ID/Touch ID/Passcode before interacting with these notifications.

Above: You can reply to a message directly from Banner notifications. The screen here shows a banner.

To Preview or Not to Preview?

You can choose whether the first line of a new text message shows up on your screen within Banners and Alerts. If you're worried about privacy,

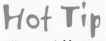

Hot Tip

Remember emoji are quickly accessible for use in messages. Simply tap the globe icon on the keyboard until you see the emoji appear. Scan or search your character of choice to add to a little character to the message.

we suggest switching this off in the Settings > Notifications > Messages section.

Lockscreen and Notification Center

If you enable Show On Lock Screen and Show In Notification Center (Settings > Notifications > select the App you want to see notifications for) you have a couple of options for interacting with new messages in these places:

- **Swipe slowly left**: This shows options to View or Clear (but you will have to unlock your phone first). In iOS 12, you can also select Manage to easily toggle the notification settings for the app without having to go to Settings.

- **3D Touch**: If you have a 3D Touch enabled iPhone (iPhone 6S and up) you 'peek and pop' by pressing firmly on notifications. This will bring up a mini view of the thread and allow you to view and reply without entering the messages app.

Above: Use 3D Touch to interact with messages without entering the app.

Hot Tip

On Face ID-enabled phones, you can preview messages just by looking at the device. When Face ID recognises you, the preview will be revealed. Enable this in Settings > Notifications > Messages and hit Show Previews When Unlocked.

MORE THAN TEXT

The Messages app is a multi-talented tool. You can also send photos, videos, GIFs, stickers, voice recordings, money, info from apps and personalised animations in Messages. We'll show you how.

Multimedia Messages

If you're sending photos and videos to fellow iPhone or iPad users, they'll be considered iMessages and will be sent over the Wi-Fi or mobile data. However, if you're sending to Android users, they'll count against your mobile contract allowances and could incur fees.

Sending Multimedia Messages

Follow the steps you would to send a normal text. In iOS 12, the method of adding a new photo is slightly different to previous versions. To pick an existing image from within a conversation thread, select the Photos icon in the bottom left corner. You'll see recent photos, but you can also select All Photos to load your gallery. To take a new photo or video select the camera icon just above it to load the camera interface.

Sharing Photos and Videos from the Photos app

You can quickly share photos and video while browsing through the

Above: Selecting the camera icon on the compose message screen presents you with the camera interface.

Hot Tip
iMessage only works between Apple devices. You can send free instant messages with your Android friends if you download WhatsApp.

Above: It's easy to transition from an iMessage thread to a FaceTime video or Audio call by tapping the contact icon.

Photos app. When viewing an image, tap on the Share icon in the bottom left (an arrow exiting a box) and this will bring up the options to share via your social networks, email and Messages. In this case, just select Messages, choose a contact and tap Send.

Receiving an MMS

Viewing MMS or picture messages is no different from reading an incoming text. The notifications and alerts follow the same principles and you'll see photos and videos you've been sent come up within the text conversation view. Small thumbnails appear in bubbles alongside normal SMS messages. A simple tap on the picture or video will blow them up to be viewable full-screen. If you like what you see, you'll also be able to download these photos and videos, by tapping the photo, pressing Share and selecting Save Image. This will save it in the Photos app.

Sending Audio Messages

If you're texting a fellow iMessage user, on the right side of the compose message field you'll see a microphone that can be used to quickly compose and send an audio message. Here's how:

1. Hold down the microphone and begin speaking. You'll see the audio meter running

Hot Tip

You can save images from the web and send them via MMS. Touch and hold an image, and you'll be given the option to save it to your Camera Roll or copy it to paste into a message or email.

across the compose message field. When you've finished speaking, release the microphone button.

2. Preview the message by pressing the play button, delete it by pressing the cross or send it by tapping the Up arrow.

Listening to Audio Messages

When Audio Messages they have been received, users can simply lift the handset to their ears in order to listen. They can also select 'Keep' in order to maintain them.

Quick Replies

How many times do you reply to messages with 'lol' or 'Haha'? Now there's an effect that offers quick reactions. Just double tap a message bubble to add a heart, thumbs up/down, haha, exclamation point or question mark. Your response will be attached to the message.

Send Messages with Effects

Begin typing the message, but before you send long press on the blue 'up' arrow. This will bring up a new screen with the option to add Bubbles and Screen effects like balloons and fireworks.

Hot Tip
Switch to the emoji keyboard by pressing the globe icon while writing a message. If the word turns yellow, you can tap it to see emoji alternatives.

Above: Hold down the microphone in the corner of the Messages app to begin recording a message. You can then send it.

Digital Touch

Digital Touch allows you to annotate quick videos and photos or send personal effects. To get started with Digital Touch open the messages app, tap the arrow to the left of the compose field and then hit the heart and two fingers icon to reveal a black screen. From here you can:

- **Quick video/photo**: Once you've entered the Digital Touch interface you tap the video camera icon. Here you'll see an capture screen with the selfie-cam enabled. Here you can tap to capture a photo/10 second video as normal, and add the following on top of them...

- **Digital touch effects**: Once the Digital Touch interface is open, you can use multi-touch gestures to send effects to other iPhone owners. These can be performed on top of the black canvas or over a photo and video. Here are the gestures: Fireball: long press; Heartbeat: tap and hold with two fingers; Heartbreak: tap, hold with two fingers and drag down; Kiss: tap with two fingers. You can also tap the coloured circle to pick a pen to scribble on your photo or video.

Above: Digital Touch enables you to annotate photos and videos with gesture-based effects.

APPS IN iMESSAGES

You can display content from apps within the conversation. Send friends a song you like from Apple Music, directions from Apple Maps, sports scores from ESPN, files from Dropbox, Movie show times from Fandango or restaurant suggestions from Yelp.

Using Apps in iMessages

To get started tap the App Store icon in the app drawer on the messages screen and choose an app from those you have installed.

1. Search for the content you wish to send and tap it to paste it into the search field.

2. Send your message as normal. The recipient will be able to interact with the content directly from the conversation.

3. If you don't see the content you wish to send, tap the App Store icon to see what's on offer. To learn how to install the app, see page 161.

Using Apps and Effects When Sending Photos

In iOS 12 Apple wants to make photos a little more playful when taking and sharing photos in the messages app. Tap the camera icon in messages and you'll see an Effects icon (it looks like a star). Below you will see a couple of examples of what you can do here, because that's much easier than explaining this silliness:

○   Add an Animoji (see page 92) on top of the actual head of your subjects.

○   Add text, filters and shapes to the photo.

○   Add stickers from apps you have installed

Above: You can add stickers to your images from a range of apps within the Messages app.

on your phone. For example, the American Airlines app lets you send attach a sticker reading 'can't wait to see you' and 'made it through security', etc.

Sending Money in iMessages

In iOS 11, Apple added the ability to quickly send money to contacts via the Apple Pay Cash feature. You'll see the Apple Pay icon in the app drawer. Tapping this allows you to select an amount and request money from or pay it to a contact. For more on Apple Pay, *see* page 156.

ANIMOJI AND MEMOJI

Forget boring old emoji, the newest iPhones with Face ID sensors offer personalised animations called Animoji and, new for iOS 12, Memoji. They can be exchanged via the iMessage app drawer.

Above: You can add an Animoji to your own head in the messages app by tapping on the Animoji icon, which looks like a monkey.

Animoji

Using the camera and depth sensors the phones can track your lips and expressions and apply it to a character like a chicken, robot or dog. They're easy and fun to create. On an iPhone X, XS, MX Max and iPhone XR running iOS 11 and up, you can quickly send an Anomoji in iMessage.

1. Open a message thread. Above the keyboard is the app draw. Select the Animoji icon, which looks like a monkey.

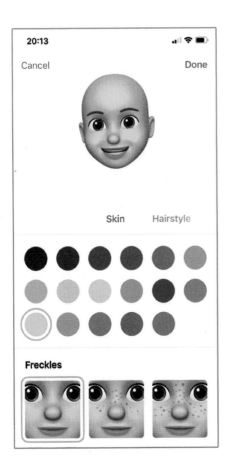

Above: In iOS 12 on Face ID-enabled phones you can create an emoji character of yourself. The iPhone captures your facial and mouth movements to create a Memoji.

2. Swipe through the various characters and tap one to select.

3. Hold the phone up so your face is in view of the sensors. When achieved a red record button will appear.

4. Hit record and begin talking. The character will mimic your facial expressions and movements. You have to 30 seconds to record.

5. When complete hit the record button again and you'll see a preview. To send hit the blue arrow, to discard hit the red trash can.

Memoji

If you thought Animoji were cool, iOS 12 brings your own personal Memoji. As the name suggests, it's an animated emoji that you can customise to look like you. Here's how to create it.

1. Select the Animoji icon from the app drawer. Swipe to the left and hit the + button.

2. Select your skin tone (and even add freckles) and swipe from right to left to select hairstyle/colour, head shape, eye shape/colour, brows, nose and lips, ears, facial hair, eyewear and headwear.

3. Select Done when complete. Your Memoji will now appear as an option whenever you select the Animoji icon from the app draw.

WAYS TO CONNECT

To access the internet, you'll need to be connected to either a Wi-Fi network or a mobile internet network. The iPhone can connect to both.

WI-FI

Wi-Fi is the wireless technology that allows you to connect to the web. The iPhone features the Wi-Fi technology similar to that on your computer or laptop, meaning you can easily access the web without physically plugging into the network:

Connecting to a Wi-Fi Network

In the first chapter, we ran through connecting to a Wi-Fi network while setting up the phone (see page 26); however, here's how to connect to a new Wi-Fi hotspot.

1. Go to Settings and select Wi-Fi. If the Wi-Fi switch is set to off, toggle it on (you can turn it on/off in the Control Center).

2. The iPhone will scan your locale for available Wi-Fi networks. After a few seconds, you'll see available networks listed under the Choose a Network header.

Right: The Wi-Fi settings screen shows which Wi-Fi networks are available.

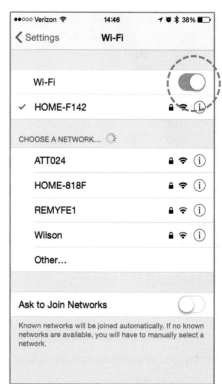

3. Select the network and, if it isn't password-protected, you'll be connected, or redirected to a screen that will enable access. The latter often happens when you log on to on public hotspot.

4. Once you're connected a blue tick will appear next to the network and the Wi-Fi icon will show in the title bar.

5. If the network is password-protected, you'll be taken to an Enter Password screen. Type this and once complete, press Join. You should now be able to access the internet. As a test, open the Safari app and attempt to load a web page.

Remembering Your Wi-Fi Places

Once you're connected to a network, your iPhone will remember you next time you're within range. So, if you connect to your home network, the iPhone will automatically pick up the signal and register your phone on the network when you get within range.

Ask to Join Networks

If you don't wish to log on automatically to a Wi-Fi network whenever you're within range, you can change this. Simply enter Settings > Wi-Fi and toggle the Ask To Join Networks switch to on. You'll then receive a notification informing you that a known network is available.

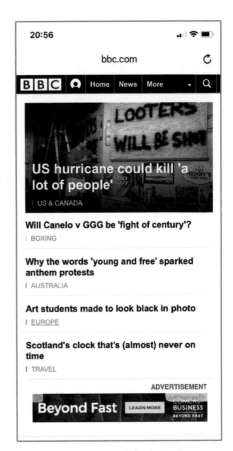

Above: Loading web pages in Safari displays them on your screen, allowing you to scroll to read text or view images.

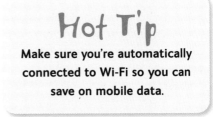

Hot Tip

Make sure you're automatically connected to Wi-Fi so you can save on mobile data.

●●○○○ Verizon 🔗   11:38   ➊ 🔋 ✱ 58% ▄▋

‹ Settings   **Wi-Fi**

Wi-Fi   ⬤

✓ Chris_wifi   🔒 🔗 ⓘ

CHOOSE A NETWORK...

2WIRE622   🔒 🔗 ⓘ

Incorrect password for "JPNET211"

Dismiss

PompanoSun-2.4   🔒 🔗 ⓘ

vladococi   🔒 🔗 ⓘ

Wilson   🔒 🔗 ⓘ

Other...

Ask to Join Networks

Above: Entering an incorrect password will prevent you from joining a Wi-Fi network.

Hot Tip

When deciding on which mobile data tariff to select, ask your network how much data you've used on average per month previously, but bear in mind that you'll probably be using more on the iPhone.

Wi-Fi Problems

Connecting to a new Wi-Fi network isn't always straightforward. Before you give up all hope of connecting via Wi-Fi, check that you have entered the password correctly (are there lower or upper case letters?) and ensure that the location you are at isn't experiencing internet problems.

Sharing Wi-Fi

Crawling around on all fours trying to read and type in a Wi-Fi password from the back of a router isn't a good look. In iOS 11, Apple introduced a neat password sharing tool. If you're at an iPhone-owning friend's house, open Settings > Wi-Fi and tap on their network ID. They should get a pop-up notification to share the password with you. Once they respond you'll see the password field magically filled. Press Done to connect.

MOBILE INTERNET

Not everywhere you go will offer access to Wi-Fi. The iPhone offers advanced mobile data connectivity, which provides over-the-air access to the internet in the same way that you're able to make calls and receive texts.

Mobile Internet Allowances

When you sign up for a mobile contract, you'll be given a mobile data allowance by your network. Cheaper monthly tariffs will only offer around 250

MB of data, which may be enough for light users. More expensive tariffs will offer upwards of 8 GB or even unlimited mobile data, which are more suited to heavy internet users.

Types of Mobile Internet

Depending on where you are, the speed of mobile internet varies a lot. In cities, you're likely to receive faster and more reliable internet connectivity than in rural areas. The current speed of your mobile internet will be reflected by the following letters and symbols in the title bar:

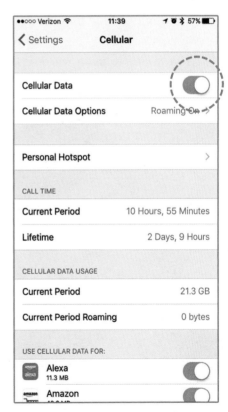

- **4G LTE**: The most advanced mobile internet speeds are now in most of the UK.

- **3G**: When 4G is not available, you'll get third-generation internet, suitable for browsing the web, watching videos, and sending and receiving email.

- **E**: In more remote locations, you may only have access to basic 2G speeds on the EDGE network.

- **No icon**: No mobile data connection is available.

Connecting to Mobile Internet

Once the iPhone is activated, it will automatically connect to mobile data networks wherever they are available. You'll never need passwords to access these, as the data comes as part of your mobile contract.

Configuring Mobile Internet

While you will be connected automatically to the mobile internet, you can still turn it off or control which apps use mobile connectivity. Enter Settings > Cellular.

Above: The mobile data screen allows you to keep track of how much data you're using. You can choose to turn off the connection by toggling from On to Off.

Here, you can toggle the Mobile Internet switch to On or Off. Beware, turning off mobile data means that browsing the web, emails and downloading apps can only be achieved over Wi-Fi.

Mobile Data Exceptions

Within the Settings > iTunes & App Store, you can control whether downloads are made over mobile data or only when using Wi-Fi. This could be important if you have a limited data contract. You can toggle the on/off perhaps when you're looking to save data.

Preserving Your Mobile Data Allowance

As explained above, most mobile contracts now offer limited data allowances per month. Here are two ways to ensure you don't incur fees by going over your allowance:

- **Use Wi-Fi**: Log on to Wi-Fi wherever possible and download large files while you're at home.

- **Stop apps refreshing**: Apps can use a lot of data when you're not using them. Go to Settings > General > Background App Refresh to stop individual apps working in the background.

Hot Tip

In Settings > Cellular you can see Cellular Data usage. If you reset this at the start of each billing cycle, you can keep track of how much you've used.

USING THE INTERNET

Now you're connected, via Wi-Fi or mobile data, you can start using your iPhone to access the internet through a web browser.

SAFARI

Safari is the web browser built in on the Apple iPhone. As it is one of the most used apps on the device, it sits neatly within the dock on the Home screen (*see page* 33). The icon is represented by a blue compass.

Loading a Web Page

To load a web page, tap the Safari icon on your Home screen. You should see a blank white page with a grey bar at the top of the screen and another at the bottom. If you've used Safari before, the last website you visited will be displayed.

1. Tap the address bar at the top-left corner of the screen, which reads 'Search or enter website name'. This will summon the keyboard. You'll also see a host of preloaded 'Favourites' like Wikipedia and YouTube, and other websites you visit regularly will be added here too. Tapping one of these will take you straight to that site.

2. Type in an internet address (e.g. bbc.co.uk and apple.com).

Above: Safari is the default web browser on the iPhone and sits in the dock.

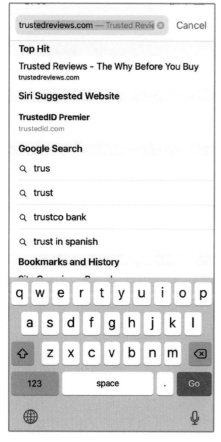

Above: Typing a search term into the Safari search bar will bring up previous related searches.

3. Press the blue Go button on the keyboard to load the web page.

3D Touch and Safari

If you have a 3D Touch enabled phone (iPhone 6S and up), you can long press on the Safari icon to get to your destination quicker. This will bring up shortcuts like new window, new private window, bookmarks and more.

Searching the Web

The address bar also allows you to search the internet. Start typing a search term (i.e. BBC Sport, Buy an iPhone) and press Search to load the Google Search results.

Finding Information Using Siri

Ask Siri a question and there's a good chance it'll find an answer from the internet within seconds – and here's how:

1. Access Siri in the usual way (see page 34).

2. Tell Siri your question, i.e. 'How tall is the world's tallest man?'

3. Siri will say 'I'm on it', 'Checking my sources' or 'Let me check'. If it can find an answer, it will load the information on a notepad, as seen in the screenshot to the right.

Searching the Internet Using Siri

If Siri cannot find an answer to your question, she will ask, 'Would you like me to search the web?' and you can tap the onscreen prompt or say, 'Yes'. This will load Bing search results for your query. Alternatively, you can just say, 'Search the web for...'. This command also works for Wikipedia.

NAVIGATING A WEB PAGE

Once you've loaded your chosen page, you can use the iPhone's responsive multi-touch screen to accomplish everything you could when using a keyboard and mouse on a PC or laptop – and a whole lot more.

Browsing a Web Page

If you're reading a news story on a web page, it's unlikely that all the text will fit on the iPhone's screen. You can browse a web page 'below the fold' by scrolling the page up, down, left or right with your finger.

Zooming into a Web Page

Unless the web page you're visiting has been optimized for viewing on a mobile screen – as has been the case for many sites – it can be quite difficult to read text and get a close look at photos without squinting. Here's how to zoom in on specific areas of the page:

Above: Siri will respond to your question by rapidly searching the internet for relevant information and loading the answer on a notepad.

1. Pinpoint the area of the page you'd like to zoom in on and place two fingers on the screen. Push outwards with both fingers until you've zoomed sufficiently and then let go of the screen.

2. The second method is to double-tap a specific area of the display quickly, which will offer a precise zoom.

Above: The SkyNews mobile website is specifically designed for mobile scrolling.

Clicking New Links

Open a link on a web page by tapping a headline or category header. The new link will load in the current window. 3D Touch comes in handy here as it can allow you to preview the content, then you can push harder to open it fully if you want.

Moving Back and Forth

To take a step back while browsing the internet, hit the Back arrow in the bottom-left corner. Then you can use the adjacent Forward arrow to travel in the other direction.

Refreshing a Web Page

You can refresh the page to display the most up-to-date information by pressing the circular arrow in the address bar, thus reloading the current page.

Mobile-optimized Websites

If a site has been optimized for mobile devices, it will automatically redirect to the mobile site when you type in the address (for example, bbc.co.uk becomes bbc.co.uk/mobile). Also, such a site will not require any zooming and content will be neatly arranged horizontally for easy scrolling.

Opening a New Web Window

To open a new web page without leaving the one you're on, just press the two windows in the bottom-right corner of the Safari page. This will show the current open windows. You can flick between these or click the + icon to start a new page. This will launch a new blank page while preserving the first page; you can have multiple windows open at any one time.

Navigating Between Multiple Web Windows

In order to switch between web windows, tap the windows icon to show a vertical carousel of cards. Swipe between them and touch the thumbnail to select that page. Users with 3D Touch phones (iPhone 6S and up) can press on the tabs to 'Peek' at them and hard press to open them fully, or 'pop' as Apple calls it.

Opening a Private Web Window

If you are, for example, searching for engagement rings, you may not want that to appear in your search history and have the surprise ruined. To protect yourself, you can follow the instructions above, but select Private. No browsing history will be recorded.

Closing a Web Window

To close a web window, select the window icon in the bottom-right corner of Safari, then individually click the crosses in the top left of each window or swipe from right to left.

Hot Tip

When viewing multiple windows, turn the phone on its side to show thumbnails of the open windows. Tap a thumbnail to open a window.

Above: To close a web page, select the window icon in the right corner of Safari, then click on the individual crosses or swipe left.

Above: Clicking the Share icon enables you to bookmark favourite websites.

Adding and Accessing Bookmarks

Bookmarks allow you to store web pages for easier access in the future. It could be a favourite website or perhaps a link to a product on a shopping site like Amazon. This is what you need to do to save a page to your Safari bookmarks:

1. Tap the Share icon above the Home button and select the Bookmark icon from the popup Share screen. From here, you can add the page to a specific Bookmark folder.

2. Press Save to add the page to your bookmarks.

3. In order to access your Bookmarks, select the open book icon at the foot of the Safari window.

4. Tap an address to open that page in the existing window.

Sharing Web Pages

Easy sharing of web content is always useful on your phone, and Safari excels at this. You'll see the Share icon (the box with an arrow leaping from it) all over the place when using the iPhone and most of these tools are available within other apps, but here are the options when you select it within Safari:

- **Mail**: The mail icon will launch the Mail client with the link copied into a new email.

- **Message**: As above, but in the Message client.

- **Twitter**: Share the link on your Twitter.

- **Facebook**: Post the link to your Facebook wall.

- **Notes/Reminders**: Add it to a note or reminder.

- **Add to Home Screen**: Adds an icon to the homepage for easy access in the future.

- **Print**: If your iPhone is configured with a wireless printer, you can print the web page.

- **Copy**: Copy the link to be shared elsewhere (into a document, a Skype conversation, alternative email app, etc.). In order to then paste the link, hold your finger down in a text box and select Paste.

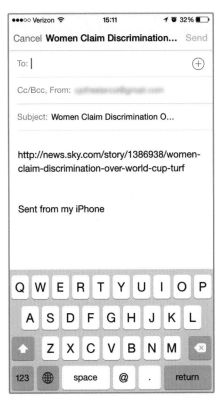

Above: By selecting the Mail icon from the Share screen, your Mail account will be launched with the web link copied into a new email.

- **Bookmark**: Saves the page to your Bookmarks.

- **Add to Reading List**: Safari offers a handy Reading List tool, which lives within the Bookmarks, allowing you to put together a list of pages you'd like to read at a later date. The Reading List screen is separated into two categories: All items and Unread items.

- **More**: Tapping this takes you to other options.

Browsing History

Bookmarks and Reading List are just a couple of ways to access familiar pages. Tapping the Bookmarks icon will give you the chance to select a History Menu, which stores information about all of the pages you've visited in the past week.

Additionally, when you start typing a website into the address bar, Safari will begin to predict the page you wish to access, based on your previous activity (for example, if you start typing Goo..., then a list of activities related to Google may appear below). If you see your preferred site, simply select it from the list.

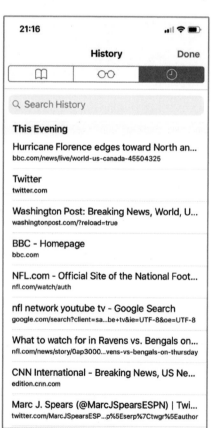

Other Web Browsers

Although Safari is the iPhone's default browser, there are other options available from the App Store (see page 160):

- **Chrome**: You can download a free mobile version for the iPhone, which features a 'tabbed browsing' feature and enables voice search.

- **Firefox**: The desktop browser made by Mozilla now has a free iPhone app available to download.

- **Edge**: If you're a Windows PC user, Edge is handy as it syncs your open web tabs to your iPhone.

Left: You can view or clear your past week's browsing history by selecting the Bookmarks icon and then History.

SOCIAL NETWORKING

Services like Twitter, Facebook, Snapchat, Instagram and many others are among the most important ways of keeping in touch with friends and our favourite celebrities, and often of keeping track of what's happening around the world.

FACEBOOK

Facebook now has over a billion users around the world. On older versions of iOS, Facebook used to be baked into the account options. These days, you have to set it up manually through the app. This means you don't get the option to sync contacts and events to your iPhone, but it does save on clutter.

Setting up Facebook

The easiest way to do this is to download the free Facebook app from the App Store and log-in using your account details. If you don't have an account, you can sign up through the app.

1. Tap the App Store icon on your Home screen and tap the search tab. Start typing Facebook and it'll appear in the suggested field. Tap Facebook.

2. Tap Get and authenticate as requested (password, Touch ID, etc.). The app will begin downloading and will appear in an open spot on your Home screen.

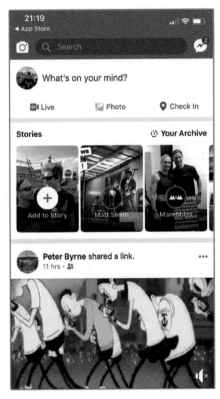

Above: The Facebook app can be donwloaded from the App Store.

3. When complete 'tap to open' and enter your login details.

Posting Using the Facebook App

A Facebook post can explain what you're doing, how you're feeling, where you are, who you're with and show a photo or video. Tap 'What's On Your Mind' at the top your news to get started.

Below: The 'What's On Your Mind' page enables you to create posts.

- **Status Update:** The empty text field allows you to type a status update. Whatever you write will be shared with your Facebook friends.

- **Add Photo/Video:** This will open the Camera Roll interface allowing you to select photos or take one to post.

- **Live Video:** Here you can broadcast live to all of your friends and interact with them as they add comments.

- **Check In:** If you'd like to alert friends to your current location (e.g. home, a favourite restaurant, sporting event), tap Check In and select from the list of nearby places.

- **Feeling/Activity:** You can tap the yellow smiley to add in how you're feeling or what you're doing (i.e. Chris Smith is drinking beer).

- **Tag Friends:** Here you can flag the post up to your Facebook friends. By tagging them you'll make sure they'll see your post as they will receive a notification.

Sharing from the Photos App

Once you've installed and logged into Facebook on your iPhone, it's easy to post photos and videos from other apps.

1. Enter the Photos app and select Camera Roll. Scroll up or down to find the photo or video of your choice and click the Share icon.

2. Select Facebook to launch the picture or video within a Facebook dialogue box.

3. If you wish, you can add a caption, tag friends, add a feeling, a location or choose who you share with.

4. Press post when done and the photo or video will upload and appear on your Facebook wall.

Sharing Web Links on Facebook

Safari makes it easy to share web pages through the Share icon at the bottom of the page. There's a dedicated Facebook button that enables you to quickly share interesting links with your friends.

Sharing to Facebook in Other Apps

As you download new apps (see page 159), you'll notice that a lot of them also incorporate the Share icon that allows you to share to Facebook. The YouTube app (see page 184) is a prime example. Other apps, such as Google Chrome, feature their own mechanisms for sharing, which also allow items to be posted to Facebook.

Hot Tip

If you don't want to install the Facebook app most of the functionality can be accessed through Facebook.com in Safari.

Below: Photos can easily be shared to Facebook by tapping the Share icon within the Photos app.

3D Touch with the Facebook App

With Facebook, 3D Touch (iPhone 6S and up) allows you to post a status, or a photo directly by pressing down on the app icon. Within the app, you can use 'peek and pop' to view links posted by friends without leaving the current page.

The Facebook News Feed

Hopefully you'll want to see what your friends are up to also! As you scroll down the screen you'll be able to interact with posts to 'Like' or comment, whereas tapping a name will take you directly to the person's profile page.

Controlling Facebook Notifications

With likes, comments, photo tags and friend requests flooding into most of our Facebook accounts, you may not want those notifications to be delivered to your phone.

1. Select Settings > Notifications > Facebook to control whether alerts appear in your Notification Center, on the lock screen and determine the type of notification you'll receive (None, Banners, etc.).

2. To receive some notifications and not others, go into the Settings menu within the Facebook app and select Notifications > Mobile.

Above: Using 3D Touch on the Facebook app enables shortcuts to write posts, upload photos and more.

TWITTER

For those unacquainted with Twitter, it is a free social network that enables more than 300 million users to post updates of 280 characters or fewer.

Setting Up Twitter

Setting up Twitter is a very similar process to enabling Facebook. Download the app from the App Store and log in or create a new account by following the on screen steps. As well as sending out tweets, you need the Twitter app to read other people's posts, receive notifications, reply to tweets and direct messages, and control who you follow.

Sending a Tweet

Once you've installed the app you can start sharing your 280-character pearls of wisdom with the world. When you've opened the app, you can confirm your identity and your timeline will load. In the top-right corner, you'll see the paper and quill icon. Tap this to begin composing your tweet and press Tweet when you're done. You can also:

- **Take a Photo/Video**: Tap the camera icon to open the capture interface and take a photo/video to add to the tweet.

- **Stream a Live Video**: Hit 'Live' to start streaming a live video.

- **Add an Image/Video**: Tap the photo icon if you want to add an existing image/video.

Above: You can share photos via Twitter by selecting the Share icon in the Camera Roll or the photo icon on the Twitter app.

- **GIF:** Tap the GIF icon to add a moving image.

- **Add a Poll:** Tap the list icon to add a poll.

- **GPS:** Tag your location by tapping the GPS pin.

Mentioning Other Users in Tweets

To 'mention' another Twitter user within your tweet, type the @ symbol on the keyboard and begin typing their username (e.g. @flametreetweet) without a space. As you type, the names of people (starting with those you follow) will appear to match your keystrokes. Tap their name to select them. When other users are 'mentioned' in tweets, they will be notified.

Navigating the Twitter App

We've covered sending a tweet, attaching photos and mentioning other users, but there's plenty more you can do with the app. It has four sections listed in the navigation bar at the bottom, as described below.

- **Home:** The main page, this displays your Twitter feed showing posts from those you follow. Pressing Home again will take you to the top of your feed.

- **Notifications:** A list of replies and mentions of your username made by other users.

- **Search:** Find users, tweets, view trending topics

Hot Tip

Adding a hashtag (e.g. #StarWars) to your tweets will mean they will appear to all users around the world when they search for a particular topic. It's a great way to join the global conversation.

Above: The Twitter app displays your Twitter feed in an easily readable and scrollable format.

and view news tailored to your interests.

○ **Messages**: Send and receive private direct messages.

Managing Twitter Notifications

Once you've installed the Twitter app, you'll receive notifications when another user replies to your tweets, retweets or favourites one of your postings, or sends you a direct message. These notifications can be configured, opened and read in the same way as Facebook ones.

Above: It is easy to add a new tweet using the Twitter app.

OTHER SOCIAL NETWORKS

The App Store offers dedicated portals to access some of the other more popular social networks (for a detailed guide to downloading apps, *see page 160*).

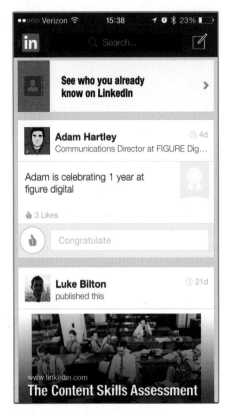

Above: Use your LinkedIn app to connect and network with fellow professionals.

Hot Tip

If you're adverse to the thousands of replies your celebrity status merits, you can turn everything off through Settings > Notifications > Twitter.

○ **LinkedIn**: This professional social network allows you to showcase your CV and to connect with colleagues and potential employees.

○ **Instagram**: A 'photo blog' to show off your best photos to your family, friends and followers. It also has lots of filters to enhance your pictures as well as stories, which allow you to share small details of your day that will disappear after 24 hours.

○ **Pinterest**: An alternative social network that simply allows users to 'pin' picture-based objects from around the web to their own 'boards'. It's great for creative types looking to collate ideas, shopaholics and lovers of funny cat pictures.

○ **Snapchat**: An app that allows users to send pictures, videos and messages to each other that disappear after a preset amount of time.

○ **Tinder**: Looking for a date? Tinder is a social network for singles and has become widely used. Swipe right to like and swipe left to pass. If someone you've liked swipes right on you too, you'll be able to exchange messages.

EMAIL

In this section, we'll talk you through the basics of setting up your various email accounts and the intricacies of sending and receiving emails using the iPhone's Mail app.

THE MAIL APP

Email is one of the iPhone's absolutely key pieces of functionality, and most users will use it several times a day. As such, Apple has taken the liberty of placing the Mail app in the dock on the Home screen, meaning it's always easily accessible. Select the app and let's get you set up.

SETTING UP YOUR EMAIL USING MAIL

Whether you're a Gmail, Hotmail, Yahoo! Mail or Microsoft Exchange user, the Mail app has got you covered. When you first select Mail, it will ask you to set up an account and you'll see the screenshot to the left. Select the provider of your choice to move to the next step.

Configuring Microsoft Exchange

The iPhone is increasingly becoming the smartphone of choice for business users and, as such, it's easy to get your work email set up on the device.

1. Select Microsoft Exchange from 'Welcome to Mail'.

2. Enter your work email address and the password you use to access it. Fill in the description field ('Work' would make sense) and press Next.

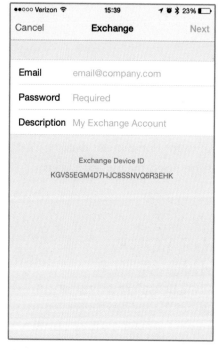

Above: Access work emails from your iPhone by setting up Exchange.

3. Once the iPhone has verified the login information, you'll need some information from your IT guys to complete the setup. Ask them for the Server information (e.g. server.company.com), your company's domain name and the username you use for the account. Once you've entered that information into the respective fields, press Next.

4. If you've done this correctly, you'll see ticks appear next to all of the fields.

5. The next screen you see features the opportunity to add information from your account to the Contacts and Calendars applications. There's more on this in the Calendars and Contacts sections (*see* pages 47 and 56).

6. Once you're happy with this, press Save and you're done.

7. Within seconds, you should see a batch of emails arrive in your inbox. If you have a lot of emails they may take a little while to all come through. Once they have, you're ready to start using your account.

Configuring Gmail, Hotmail, Yahoo! and Others

If adding Microsoft Exchange email details seemed a little tricky and convoluted, don't worry, because setting up your personal webmail email is a doddle.

1. Select your email provider from the list on the 'Welcome to Mail' screen.

2. If you've added a different account already, you'll need to select Settings > Mail, Contacts, Calendar > Add Account.

3. To configure the likes of Gmail, Yahoo!, Hotmail and others, add your name, email address, password and a description (this is optional, but if you have several email accounts it's a good idea to put a name in here), and press Next.

4. If you've entered the details correctly, ticks will appear next to all of the fields and the iPhone will progress to the final setup screen.

5. Once that's dealt with, press Save to start receiving emails as normal. You'll also be asked whether you want to sync your contacts, calendar information and any reminders you've set using that service. This can be useful to do.

Hot Tip

If you have too many unread emails and you want to turn off the red badges go to Settings > Notifications > Mail, tap your account and toggle badges off.

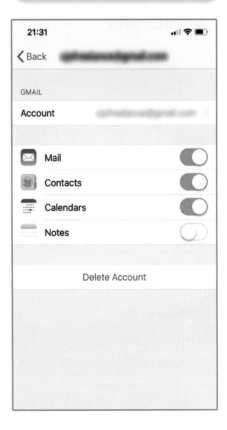

Above: Once you have configured your account to the Mail app, you can sync details such as contact lists.

Syncing Email with Other Apps

Depending on which email provider you use, you'll be able to pull in details to work with some of the other apps on the iPhone. For example, Yahoo! users can sync their Contacts and Calendars, as well as their Reminders and Notes (see chapter one, page 12). Head to Settings > Passwords & Accounts (in iOS 12) to turn these settings on and off.

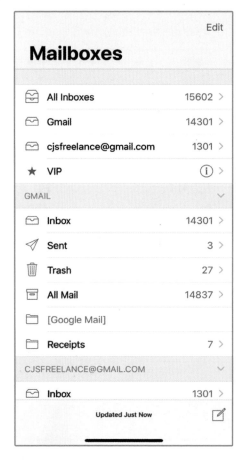

Above: The Mailboxes screen allows you to view your accounts individually or through a combined inbox.

Combined and Multiple Inboxes

Once you've added your accounts, you can access them through the Mailboxes screen within the Mail app (see screenshot left). Here, you'll see the option to select All Inboxes, which will show you all emails in the same inbox, regardless of which of your configured email addresses they were sent to. This can be hugely helpful if you have various different email accounts. You can also select each inbox individually to see segregated Exchange, Gmail, Yahoo!, etc. accounts.

Email VIPs

The final option on the Mailboxes screen is to view emails from your VIPs (bosses, best friends, significant other, your mum etc.). Select VIP from the Mailboxes and choose a specific contact from the Contacts app. These VIPs will have their own specific inbox, and you can easily configure special notification settings for their emails, to maker sure you see them, by using the VIP Alerts button.

DEALING WITH EMAIL

Sending and receiving emails using the Mail app is just as easy as text messaging.

Sending Email

Here's a quick step-by-step guide to firing off your first email:

1. Open the Mail app and select the New Message icon in the bottom-right corner of the screen.

2. Choose your recipient by typing the address into the 'To' field (known contacts will be suggested as you type); for example, joe.bloggs@email.com.

3. To select a recipient from your Contacts, press the + icon and select from the list.

4. Click Subject and type an email subject (e.g. Dinner?).

5. Tap the main body of the email, which usually says Sent from my iPhone, to begin typing.

6. Once you've finished typing, press Send in the top right corner. You'll hear a 'whoosh' sound once the email is sent.

Hot Tip

While 'peeking' at an email with 3D Touch you can slide left to reveal a trash icon. Once this icon turns red, you can release to delete the email.

Above: Choose a recipient, enter body text and select Send in the top right-hand corner to send a new email.

Above: Attach a photo by holding your finger in the main section and selecting 'Insert Photo or Video'.

Attaching Pictures or Video

Here is how to include an image or video in an email:

1. Hold your finger down anywhere within the body text field to summon a pop-up menu that says Select, Select all, Paste.

2. Press the arrow to the right of that menu and select Insert Photo or Video.

3. Touch a photo from the Camera Roll to launch a preview and press Choose if you're happy. This will attach the photo to the email. Repeat these steps to add multiple photos.

4. Touch the screen to place the cursor above or below the photo to continue typing your email.

5. Alternatively, you can press the Share button within the Photos app and choose one or multiple photos to load those photos pre attached to a new email.

Sending an Email Using Siri

As with Facebook, Twitter and Messages, you can dictate an email to Siri to save typing it.

1. Launch Siri and say 'Send an email to...', including your recipient's name. Siri will load an applicable person from your Contacts.

Above: Siri can be used to send emails to people listed in your contacts.

2. You'll be asked for a subject line and text, which you can dictate to Siri. She will then ask whether you want to send it or cancel it.

3D Touch in Mail

Again, 3D Touch proves its worth. You can press down on the Mail icon on the Home screen to see quick actions like 'New Message', 'Search' and more if you have 3D Touch (iPhone 6S and up). When you're in the inbox you can press down on the display to 'peek' at an email in your inbox, and swipe up to reveal actions like Reply. Or you can press harder on an email to pop it open.

Multitasking with Mail

As with all iPhone apps, you return to an app at the precise place where you left it. So, if you need to leave the Mail app while composing an email, you can safely browse to another app without losing your draft. When you return to the app, your half-composed email will be waiting for you.

Saving Drafts

Alternatively, you can easily save draft emails until you return to them later. When composing an email, press Cancel in the top-left corner of the screen. From the pop-up menu, you can choose Delete Draft to discard, Save Draft to add it to the Drafts folder or Cancel to continue composing the email.

Above: Swiping down an email message minimizes the window at the foot of the app.

Receiving Push Email

The default setting for the Mail app is to bring in new emails as they arrive. This is called 'Push email' and it is designed so that it will continually go to ask the server if there are new emails, rather than the user having to refresh manually. When you receive a new email, you'll usually be notified by a sound (the 'ding' sound is the default) and a visual alert. A number next to the Mail icon on the Home screen will also show up new emails.

Fetch Email

While Push email arrives automatically, Fetch email instructs the Mail app to check for new arrivals at regular intervals. This can save battery if you're running low. Select Settings > Passwords & Accounts > Fetch New Data. Turn Push off and select from the options under Fetch. You can choose every 15, 30 and 60 minutes or Manually (you'll only be notified of new emails when you open the app). Regardless of these settings, every time you open the Mail app, it will check for new emails.

Notify Me

The Notify Me feature ensures you receive a notification on the lock screen if you're particularly keen to see a reply to that thread. When composing tap the bell within the subject line and select Notify Me. This helps to ensure you see the emails that really matter.

Scheduling Email Updates

Come 5 p.m. you may not want work emails but would still like to be notified of received personal emails. You can use the Do Not Disturb settings to good effect here, but here's what to do to schedule when the Mail app searches for new emails:

1. Select the Settings app and Passwords & Accounts.

2. Select Fetch New Data and choose the account in question.

3. Scroll down and select Manually. This will only bring in new email when you manually enter the Mail app.

4. When it's time to go to work, follow the steps above and change the schedule to Push.

Refreshing Email

You can manually load new emails at any time. From any of the menu pages (Accounts, Inbox, Sent, etc.), you can refresh by placing your finger on the screen and pulling down until the spinning wheel appears at the top. At the

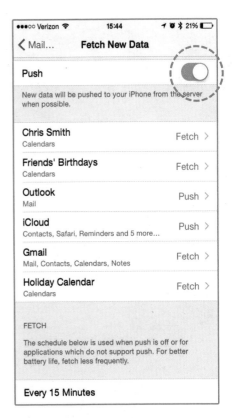

Above: You can choose whether you receive your emails by Push or Fetch. Choosing the Fetch option saves battery.

foot of the page, you'll see a message telling you when the folder or Inbox was last updated (e.g. Updated 13/09/17 12:35 PM).

Reading Emails

When you open the Mail app and select your Inbox, you'll see all emails listed with the sender, subject, first three lines of text and sent time. Any unread emails will be represented by a blue dot to the left of the message. Touching the preview will open the email. Touching the Inbox arrow in the top-left navigation bar will take you back there, whereas hitting the up or down arrows will take you to the previous/next email in the list.

Selecting Web Content from Email

Many emails will feature web links, perhaps from colleagues, friends or shopping sites, that require you to click to view more content. You can tap a hyperlinked picture or a line of text and the web page will instantly open within the Safari browser. With 3D Touch on the iPhone 6S and up, you can preview these links by pressing down on the screen.

Replying to, Forwarding and Managing Emails

After reading an email, use the menu at the bottom of the screen to decide what to do next. The blue menu at the foot of the app gives you several options:

- **Flag**: Add a flag to the email to signal its importance or mark it as unread.

- **Folder**: Click this icon to move the email to a new folder (e.g. Receipts, Trash).

- **Bin/Archive**: Discard the email by removing it from your inbox and sending it to the Trash or your archives.

- **Reply**: The arrow allows you to Reply, Reply All, Forward it to a new contact or Print the email (if your iPhone is configured with a Wi-Fi printer).

- **New Message**: From anywhere within the Mail app, you can hit the New Message icon to begin typing an email.

Above: After selecting the arrow icon from the bottom of an email, the reply screen will be displayed. You can then choose to Reply, Forward or Print. If there are images attached, you'll be able to save those too.

Deleting Emails

There are bound to be plenty of emails that you don't wish to read or store. Here's what you need to do to dispose of them:

1. Select Edit from within your inbox and an empty circle will appear next to all emails. Touching this circle will highlight it with a blue tick.

2. Highlight all of the emails you'd like to delete.

3. Tap the blue 'Trash' button at the bottom right of the screen.

4. From here, you can also Move emails to new folders and Mark them for further attention.

Mail Folders, Drafts and Trash

Not all of your email activities take place within your main Inbox. There will be times when you'll want to access your Sent Mail, Draft emails and perhaps emails within your Trash that were deleted prematurely. From the Mailboxes page, select from the Accounts menu. This will take you to a list of folders where you can access Drafts, Sent Mail, Spam, Trash and more.

Conversation View

If you've received multiple emails from the same sender on the same subject (if you've replied and they've replied, and so on), you'll see a number in a square box to the right of the message preview. Selecting these emails will bring up a new page with previews of all of the emails associated with that conversation.

Mail Gestures

As well as 3D Touch in there are other gestures you can to manage email. You can move emails to different folders and perform a number of other actions by swiping the message preview left or right.

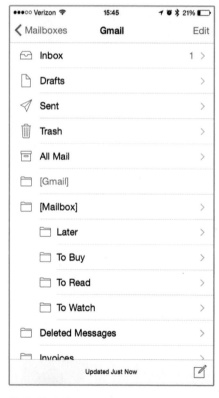

Above: The Folders screen allows you to organize and easily access different folders in your emails.

- **Short swipe from right to left**: This will present three options; Archive/Trash (depending on your email provider), Flag and More. More gives you a shortcut to Reply, Forward, Mark as Unread, Move to Junk, etc.

- **Long swipe from right to left**: A pronounced swipe will send the email to the archive or delete it depending on which provider you're using.

- **Swipe from left to right**: This will give you the option to mark the email as read.

- **Customize**: You can customize these options in Settings > Mail, Contacts, Calendars. Scroll down to the Mail subhead and select Swipe Options.

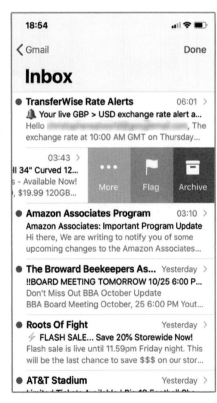

Above: Swiping message previews left and right enables a number of options like Trash, Archive, Flag and More.

CALENDAR

Back in the first chapter, we introduced the iPhone's built-in Calendar app; however, to make the best use of it, it's better to have all of your email and social networking accounts set up, which we have done in the previous pages.

Above: The Calendar app will display today's date on the Home screen (here, it is second from the left, top row).

THE CALENDAR APP

This app sits on your Home screen. Touch it to see a monthly grid view, displaying the month, the year and an icon for every day in the month. Today's date will be highlighted in red. Tapping the date will show you a schedule for the day, including any birthdays synced from Facebook.

Navigating the Calendar App

Touching another date icon in the monthly view will take you directly to that day and show the appointments you have listed then. Touching an event will provide more details, such as the time, location, invitees and more.

○ **Back arrow:** The arrow in the top-left corner allows you to move back to the month or the year view.

○ **List view:** This option displays the month, and events for each day listed beneath.

Above: Touching a date in the calendar app brings up details of appointments entered for that day.

○ **Search**: This lets you browse for calendar events.

○ **Add new event**: *See page 136.*

○ **Today**: Hitting this option in the bottom-left corner will always take you back to Today.

○ **Calendars**: Tap this to choose which of your Calendar accounts are displayed within the app (Gmail, iCloud, Friends' Birthdays, etc.)

○ **Inbox**: Here will sit any invitations you get to events, meetings or parties, etc. You can acknowledge them, accept or decline here.

Above: If you turn off the Calendar for a particular account, it will be removed from your phone.

Hot Tip

When viewing the calendar in monthly view, days with events scheduled will have a black dot underneath the date.

Configuring Multiple Calendars

By default, the Calendar app features All Calendars. This means that it will feature events from all the accounts you've given the Calendar app permission to access (e.g. Mail, Notes, Messages etc.). When setting up your email, you would have been asked whether you wanted it to sync with the Calendar app (see page 120). To select which accounts send events to the Calendar app, select Settings > Accounts & Passwords, then choose an account (e.g. iCloud, Gmail, Exchange) and switch the Calendar button to on or off.

Family Calendars

If you have enabled Family Sharing, you'll see a new Family Calendar created within the app. Tap Calendars, scroll down and you'll see it listed with your other calendars as Family. This links all members of the family. Users can also send Reminders to the whole family so they don't miss movie night! You can of course turn this off by unchecking the tick.

Hot Tip

Upcoming calendar appointments and reminders will appear in the Today screen under the 'Up Next' heading. This is an easy way to see your schedule for the day. Tapping the event will also allow you to interact with it.

iCloud Calendars

One of the coolest and most useful iCloud features is the Calendar functionality, which syncs across multiple Apple devices. Therefore, if you make an entry on your iPhone, you'll see it on your Mac computer, iPad and even on the web-based iCloud.com page. To enable the iCloud Calendar, go to Settings > iCloud and turn Calendars on.

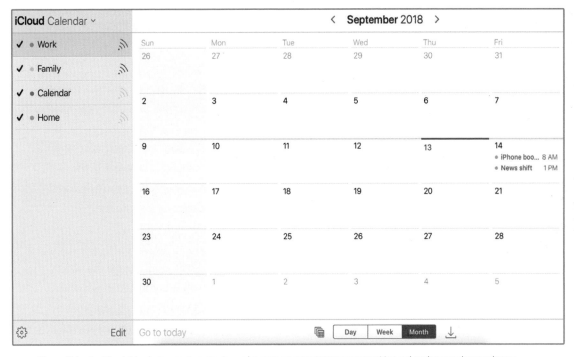

Above: Using the iCloud Calendar is a great way to view and manage your appointments on your Mac, and can be synced across devices.

Viewing Multiple Calendars

If you've configured multiple email accounts, you can choose to view them all or just one at a time from the app's Calendars setting. Pressing the various items in the list (e.g. iCloud Home, Family) will add/remove a tick, making it visible/invisible in the All Calendars screen.

Searching Your Calendar

With all of these accounts pushing data to and from the iPhone app, it can be difficult to keep track. To search for details of a certain event, you can use the Search Calendars bar near the top of the app; tap and type to see events.

ADDING TO THE CALENDAR

The iPhone Calendar app will automatically sync with your various email and iCloud accounts (more on that later), but you can also add items manually – here's how:

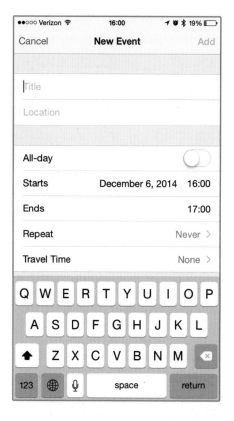

1. Open the Calendar app and hit the + button in the top-right corner.

2. From the new Add Event screen, enter the Name and Location of the event in the fields provided. By Location, you'll be asked to input an address or just use the Current location.

3. If this is an all-day event, toggle the switch to on. If not, select the Starts/Ends menu from the Add Event screen to add times by using the scroll wheel. You can also add a Time Zone, or choose to repeat the event. You can also build in necessary Travel Time.

4. Select Add to save the event within the Calendar app.

Left: Add an event to your Calendar by using the keyboard to enter the title, location and times. You can also choose to receive an alert.

5. Go to the date of the event to see it.

6. Tap the event to see the Event Details.

Adding a Calendar Event Using Siri

Part of Siri's remit is to manage your Calendar, meaning that you can add appointments to your Calendar app and invite attendees in a couple of seconds. For example, you can launch Siri and say, 'Schedule meeting with Joe Bloggs at Starbucks at 5 p.m. on Friday.' If you confirm this meeting with Siri, it will be added to your Calendar app and an invitation will be sent to your recipient. You can also cancel appointments in the same way by saying, 'Cancel appointment with...'

Setting an Alert for a Calendar Event

Any Calendar app worth its salt will alert you when the event is approaching. When adding or editing (select the event and press Edit) an event, you can customize when you will receive an alert and select anything from None to a day before. You can also set a second alert closer to the time.

Above: You can schedule an event using Siri, who will add it to your Calendar.

Calendar Alerts in Today Screen

Calendar events are automatically configured to appear in your Today screen (with iOS 8 and up), which can be accessed at any time swiping to the farthest left homescreen. This means that the events for that day will always appear as a constant reminder throughout the day.

Above: You can invite contacts to Calendar events by selecting Add Invitees and then typing email addresses or adding them from your contacts.

Hot Tip

Every time you update the event (time, date, notes), invitees will be notified by email.

Selecting Calendar Alert Styles

You can customize how you'll be alerted to all manner of Calendar events from within Settings > Notifications > Calendar. For example, select Upcoming Events to choose the Alert Style (None, Banners or Alerts), choose whether it'll appear on the lock screen, whether it'll make a sound and show in the Notification Center.

Invite Contacts to Calendar Events

If you're planning a business meeting or a party, you can use the Calendar app to invite potential attendees.

1. From the Add/Edit Event screen, select Invitees; this will then load the Add Invitees screen, the iPhone's keyboard and a To: field.

2. To add an invitee, you can start typing the email address in the To: field. Alternatively, press the + icon to load your contacts. Selecting a contact will add them to the list.

3. Select 'Done' to send out the invites.

4. To see who has accepted, rejected or is yet to reply to the invitation, tap the event to access the Event Details screen.

Scheduling a Regular Calendar Event

If you have to go to the same meeting every week, you can schedule a repeating Calendar event. From the Add/

Edit Event screen, select the Repeat option. The default setting is Never, but you can choose Every Day, Week, Two Weeks, Month and Year (great for remembering your grandmother's birthday!).

Adding Notes to Calendar Events

To add details about the event, tap the Notes field and then use the iPhone's keyboard to type details; press 'Done' when you've finished.

Deleting an Event

To delete an event from your own Calendar (and those who may have accepted invites), select the Edit button from the Event Details page, scroll down to the bottom of the screen and hit Delete Event.

Moving/Extending an Event

You can change the details of an event by using the Edit screen, but there's an easier way too. Select the Day view in your Calendar and place your finger on the event bubble. You'll then be able to drag the event to earlier or later in the day by moving it up or down. To switch days, drag it to the left or right. When you've settled on a place, let go of the bubble. You'll also notice markers at the top and bottom of the bubble; dragging these in or out will change the length of the appointment.

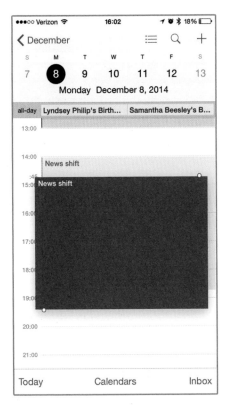

Above: In Calendar Today view you move an event by dragging the event bubble up or down manually.

LOCATING YOURSELF

Whether you're searching for directions or finding a restaurant nearby or checking in at your favourite venue, you'll use the iPhone's mapping and location services more than you think. Over the next few pages, we'll explain how to get the best out of your new personal GPS device.

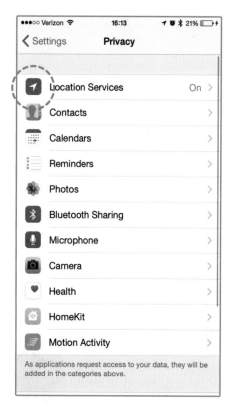

Above: You can switch on Location Services in your privacy settings.

LOCATION SERVICES

When you first set up your iPhone (*see page 25*), you will have been asked whether you wanted to enable Location Services and allow certain apps to access your geographical location. This isn't just handy for Maps but also for social networks, shopping and ticketing apps, the camera, and Siri.

How Location Services Works

The iPhone can calculate your approximate location by using the GPS signal, proximity to a mobile network tower and data from the Wi-Fi network you're logged on to. When Location Services is in operation, you'll see a compass arrow in the iPhone's title bar.

Enabling Location Services

If you switched on Location Services when setting up the phone, you're good to go; otherwise, it's easy to change. Head to Settings > Privacy and switch Location Services to On.

Enabling Location Services for Individual Apps

This is important, because there is no need to give your location to apps that don't need it. On the Settings > Privacy > Location Services screen, you'll see a list of apps requesting access to your location. Toggle the switches to Always, While Using or Never for each app.

Sharing Your Location

It can be handy to share your location with a friend. Open the Messages app along with a conversation. Tap the contact icon and select Info. From here you can select from two options: Send My Current Location (a one-off location is sent) and Share My Location (you can choose for one hour, until the end of the day or indefinitely).

APPLE MAPS APP

The Maps app brings voice-controlled, turn-by-turn navigation to the iPhone, replacing the need for a sat nav.

Opening Maps

The first time you open Maps, a graphical map will load, with a blue dot surrounded by a circle, which represents your current location.

Navigating Around Maps

You can move around the Maps app screen using a lot of the same gestures we've encountered in apps like Safari.

- **Scan:** Move around the map by placing your finger on the screen and moving it in any direction.

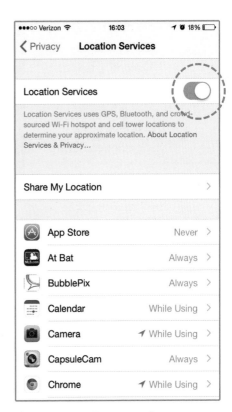

Above: The Location Services menu allows you to view and edit which apps are utilizing this service.

Hot Tip

To pinpoint your current location at any time, press the compass arrow in the top-right corner.

- **Zoom**: You can zoom in and out on any map by touching the screen with two fingers and moving them in or out. Double-tapping the screen will also zoom.

- **Landscape**: Turn your phone on its side to change the view.

Above: Turn your phone on its side to view in landscape.

Changing the Map

As well as the standard graphical view, you can also access satellite imagery. You'll see an information icon in the top-left corner allows you to switch to the satellite map or, in some areas tapping it allows you to view the Transit systems. You can also switch the view to Hybrid or Satellite, show traffic information, show the 3D map, drop a pin and even print the map.

SEARCHING FOR A LOCATION

There are a number of ways to search for a particular place (e.g. a restaurant, office, friend's house) if you're using the Maps app. Tap the search bar at the foot of the screen and begin typing. You'll begin to see suggestions as you type. In the next few pages

Above: You can view your location and directions in Satellite view.

we'll explain how to use the Direction, Search and
Bookmarks options.

Get Directions from the Maps App

After searching for the location, below the map
you'll see a blue button reading Directions and the
time it takes to get there. Tapping this will load a
new map with the start and end point.

1. Select your mode of transport at the bottom.
   There's Drive, Walk, Transit and Ride.

2. By default you will start from your current
   location. To change this tap My Location.

3. Below the Map are the time of journey, address
   and a Go button to enter navigation. Before
   tapping this check your route.

4. If applicable, a deep blue line will appear
   showing the route and potential traffic in
   yellow and red, depending on the severity.
   This will be the fastest route.

5. In a lighter blue you'll see alternative routes,
   each giving you an estimate of how long it
   takes. You can tap on them to switch.

6. You can use the blue dot to navigate your
   own way or press the green Go button to

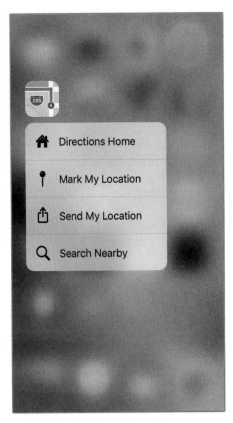

Above: If you use 3D Touch on the Maps icon,
you can ask the app to take you straight home.

**Tap the 'i' on the main Maps
page at any time to changes
the settings to show Transport,
Satellite or Mark My Location.**

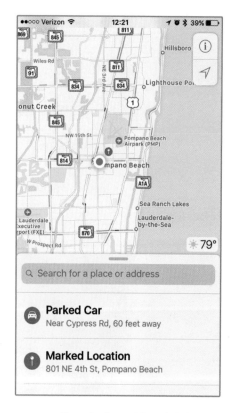

Above: Tap the search bar to find a location

launch voice-controlled, turn-by-turn navigation (*see* page 145).

Finding a Place

Selecting the Search bar in the Maps app is the simplest way to find what you're looking for. The new Maps app in iOS aims to give you a helping hand if you're in a new area.

1. Tap the bar and begin typing your request. It can be an address or the name of a place, venue, restaurant, etc.

2. Familiar locations and suggestions based on what you've typed will appear, as well as encircled options.

Above: After searching for a location you'll see further information like opening hours, reviews and photos.

Hot Tip

In Settings > Maps you can set your preferred transport type, whether your distances are measured in miles or kilometres and turn Show Parked Location on and off.

You can tap Food, Drinks, Shopping, Travel, Services, Fun, Health and Transport. Tap a suggestion or continue typing and press Search.

3. The nearest result (if you search for McDonald's, there'll be lots!) will appear in the center of the map.

4. To get directions to the place you've chosen, starting at your Current Location, tap the blue Directions bar unerneath the name and then press Go to commence turn-by-turn navigation (see page 145).

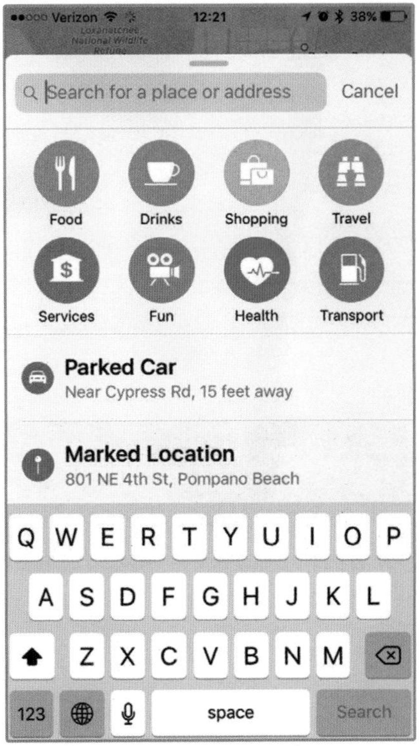

Search Options

When you search for a location using Maps, you can swipe up on the page that appears next to the result. This will display more details about the location, such as full address and phone number (if applicable), a star rating, photos, as well as the option to get directions to and from the location or add it to a contact.

Above: Apple Maps offers helpful suggestions and shortcuts to nearby amenities. For example, tap Fun and then Cinemas to see a list of cinemas nearby.

Directions to Favourites, Recent, Contacts

Tap the search bar to reveal a list of suggestions. Here, you can select from Favourites (see below), Recents (recent places you've searched for) and places nearby. Select any of these to view them on the map and then press 'Start' to begin navigation.

Interacting with Your Location

To save a place to your Favourites list, hold down a finger on the display or search for the place. Swipe up to reveal the menu, scroll down and select Add To Favourites. Here you can also create or add to an existing contact or choose to share the location via Messages, Notes, Facebook, etc. You can also choose to Mark My Location.

Sharing a Location

The Share icon appears when you search. Tap it to see options like Message, Mail etc. You can also share your location from the Messages app (see page 139).

Parked Car

Maps will remember where you parked your car. Once your journey is complete, the iPhone will automatically remember where you parked. It'll also give you a notification that will guide you back to it.

Dropping a Pin

If you're browsing in Maps, you can hold your finger down on the screen to drop a pin on a place you want to visit. An address bar will pop up with the option to get directions.

Marked Location
1.1 mi

Edit Location

Directions
5 min drive

Kestler Field
801 NE 4th St
Pompano Beach, FL 33060
United States

Above: When browsing using Maps you can drop a pin to view directions to a chosen location.

Get Directions Using Siri

Siri is integrated with the Maps app to allow you to load directions. Hold down the Home button and request directions to a location; you can say, 'Directions home' and the Maps app will load with turn-by-turn navigation.

Left: Use Siri to help you find your way; simply launch Siri and ask for directions to where you want to go. A turn-by-turn directions screen will immediately start.

MAPS' TURN-BY-TURN NAVIGATION

Remember that Go button we discussed? Just like an in-car sat nav unit (e.g. a TomTom), the app will guide you from your current location to your destination with a series of detailed audio and visual instructions.

Using Turn-by-Turn Navigation

Press Go from any Directions page (see page 141) and follow these instructions:

1. Once you hit Go, the iPhone will issue its first voice command (e.g. 300 feet turn left on to Castle Street), while a visual road sign will display the same message.

2. Your position will be illustrated by a moving compass icon, which will move as you do. As you get close to your next turn, the command will be repeated.

Hot Tip

In order to navigate to your home address from wherever you are, tap the search bar and select Home.

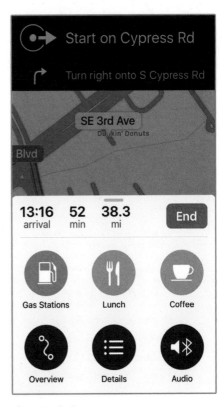

Above: Turn-by-Turn navigation is accompanied by voice instructions.

Hot Tip

The iPhone's multitasking skills allow you to leave the app and still receive voice instructions. When you leave, the title bar will flash green with the message 'Touch to return to Navigation'.

Above: The Compass feature is a useful way of getting your bearings.

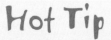

Hot Tip

If you're searching for somewhere to eat with Maps, why not download the Open Table app? This will enable you to make reservations directly from the listing in Maps.

3. When you're on the next street, you'll be told how long to continue for.

4. The next instruction will appear in visual form on the screen. Follow these instructions until you reach your destination. Once you're at your destination, press End.

Viewing Written Directions

To get a written summary of the directions, tap the tab showing your estimated arrival time. Tap Details to see the instructions in a list or an overview of the journey on the map. Text is nice and large so you can see while the phone is stowed on a dash mount. Tapping this will also enable you to reroute to get petrol or food.

Catch a Ride

Like Messages, Maps integrates third-party apps in iOS 10 and up. If ridesharing apps like Uber are available in your area, you can use them to book a ride directly from the Maps app. Once you've searched for directions (see page 143), you can tap 'Ride' to see the options and, if you're signed up for the ride sharing service, book as you would normally.

Enabling the Compass

While hitting the Compass icon once in the top-right corner will take you directly to your Current Location, holding it down will load the full compass. As you turn, the map will turn with you with the direction you're going in pointing to the top of the screen, making it easy to tell whether you're moving in the right direction.

3D Maps and Flyovers

For certain cities, you'll be able to take a Flyover tour of the area. Where it is available, you will see a 'Flyover Tour' tab next to the Directions button after you have searched for a place (San Francisco has it, for example). Tap this to start the tour.

You can also view some places in 3D by dragging two fingers up the screen. This works best in the Satellite view.

Above: The 3D Map view allows you to get greater perspective. Especially of landmarks like Big Ben.

Other Maps Options

Apple Maps is a great tool. But it is always useful to have other options that have different benefits.

Google Maps

You can download Google Maps from the App Store free of charge. The app offers fantastic voice search, turn-by-turn directions and the impressive Street View tech.

Waze

Also owned by Google, Waze is a great app that is also free on the App store. It uses continually updated user

Golden Gate Bridge

Above: Apple's flyover feature allows you to browse the cityscapes of cities.

contributions to warn of traffic conditions, accidents on the road, speed cameras and police traps.

Traditional Sat Nav Providers

Afraid that smartphones were putting them out of business, the likes of TomTom and Garmin have launched iPhone apps with advanced features such as live traffic updates, regular map updates and advanced lane guidance. Search for Maps on the App Store to find these apps.

USES OF LOCATION IN OTHER APPS

As explained earlier in this section, the Locations Services is useful beyond map apps – here are some of our favourites.

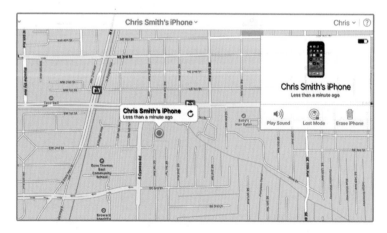

○ **Find My iPhone:** This service enables you to use another device (an iPad, Mac computer or iCloud. com) to locate a missing or lost phone on a map, make it play a sound, remotely lock or erase it to protect your data. (Go to Settings > Location Services > Find My iPhone).

- **Checking in**: Apps such as Facebook and Twitter and a host of others (*see page 119*) encourage you to use Location Services to 'check in' at a location.

- **Exploring an area**: Many apps (Open Table, Yelp, Foursquare, etc.) use location data to let you know what's in your area, e.g. restaurants, hotels, attractions, petrol stations and cash machines.

- **Entertainment**: Apps such as Movies by Flixster and Ticketmaster use your location to bring you details of events nearby.

- **Geo-tagging**: The iPhone's Camera app (and third-party apps like Instagram) add a geographical location to your snaps. The location data will be identified in the Moments section of the Photos app. Tap the place name to load the location on a map.

Above: Check in on the Facebook app to interact with others and keep friends updated on your whereabouts.

Hot Tip

If you've enabled Family Sharing through iCloud, you'll be able to track the location of your family members' linked devices. You can also start sharing locations, so it's easier to keep tabs on everyone.

BUILT-IN APPS

The iPhone comes with a host of built-in, or 'native', apps. From Maps and Siri to Mail and FaceTime video calling, there are plenty of tools to make life easier.

Above: The Apple News app aggregates content from all of your favourite news sources.

COMES WITH...

The iPhone 'native' apps are the backbone of your iPhone user experience. Here are the main ones:

○ **Calendar, Phone, Clock, Notes and Reminders**: Great organizational apps.

○ **Camera**: The Camera app works with the iPhone's built-in cameras to shoot stills and record HD video.

○ **Contacts**: This app is your address book. It's a store for the phone numbers, addresses and contact information of all your friends, family and colleagues.

○ **FaceTime**: Apple's built-in video calling app that lets you chat face-to-face with other iOS and Mac users.

○ **Health**: This app gives you an easy-to-read dashboard of your health and fitness data. If you have an iPhone 5S and up, it'll also track your steps (*see page 154 for more information*).

- **iTunes Store, Books and App Store**: Find new content via these store portals.

- **Mail/Messages**: Essential communications tools for staying in touch with friends, family and colleagues.

- **Maps**: Get yourself from A to B, whether driving or on foot, with Apple Maps.

- **Music, Video and Photos apps**: These apps let you manage your multimedia content.

- **News**: The Apple News app is a great way to keep up with updates from your favourite publications.

- **Pages, Keynote, Numbers**: Apple's own versions of Microsoft Office are now built into the iPhone.

- **Safari**: This is the iPhone's standard web browser. You can also auto-sync bookmarks and favourites across iOS devices.

- **Siri**: Apple's voice assistant. This app lets you issue instructions and tackle tasks using voice commands.

- **Wallet**: Designed to help manage boarding passes, coupons, tickets and gift cards by keeping them all stored in a scannable digital format in the app.

- **Weather**: Get hourly, daily and weekly forecasts for multiple locations.

Above: Apple's Wallet app allows you to keep all your debit cards, store cards and tickets.

ADDITIONAL SERVICES

Apple wants the iPhone to be so much more than a simple smartphone. It wants the device to be responsible for monitoring your health, for paying for goods and services and much more.

APPLE HEALTH

The Health app aims to provide a comprehensive picture of your health. There are so many potential uses here, but we'll focus on the basic ones.

Setting up the Health App

The Health app is represented by a heart on a white background. When you first open the app, you'll need to set up some personal details.

Adding a Medical ID

Next you'll be asked to create a Medical ID. Here, you can add vital information like your medical conditions, medication, organ donor status, emergency contact etc. If you add a Medical ID, you can also ensure it appears in the Emergency dial section of the phone so it can be accessed with the phone locked.

Enabling Apps to Work with Health

The main Health Data screen shows four major options: Activity, Mindfulness, Nutrition and Sleep.

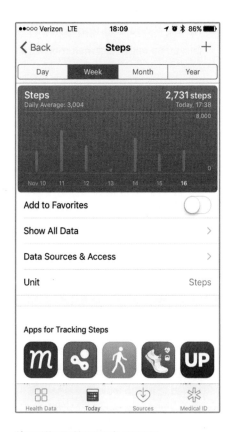

Above: The Health app tracks your steps, flights of stairs climbed and much more.

Depending on whether you're using any apps that collect data of this ilk, you'll see different results. These screens also recommend apps you can install to build up this picture. When using these apps you may be asked whether you want to enable Apple Health access. Otherwise it can be enabled within settings.

- **Activity**: Data from an app like Runkeeper can by synced with Health.

- **Mindfulness**: Mindful minutes can be tracked through usage of apps like 10% Happier.

- **Nutrition**: Using the Lifesum app to track your diet? It can report back to Health.

- **Sleep**: The Pillow app tracks your sleep and will report data back to the Health app.

SCREEN TIME

Apple wants you to use your iPhone less. The Screen Time app shows how long you spend using various apps and services with the idea of assisting your digital wellbeing.

Screen Time Data

Screen Time is logged automatically in iOS 12. Head to Settings > Screen Time to see the dashboard. It'll tell you how long you've been actively on your phone that day, split into categories like social networking and health.

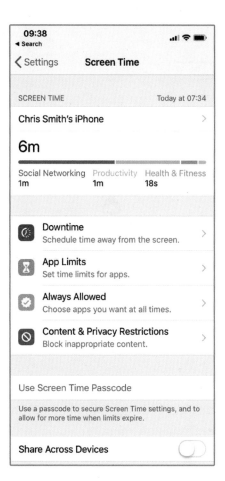

Above: The Screen Time dashboard shows you how, and how long you've been using your phone on any given day and for the last week.

Downtime

Tap Settings > Screen Time > Downtime and tap start and end to schedule time away from the screen. For example, in order to get a good night's sleep you might wish to stop using your phone at 8pm. Only apps you choose to allow can be used.

Above: If you've used up your allotted Screen Time. Opening an app will display this screen.

App Limits

Spend too much time on social networks? Here you can limit yourself. Select App Limits > Add Limit to choose Social Networking from the list. Adjust the time to set your limit. After this time has elapsed the app icon will be greyed-out with an hourglass next to it. Tapping the icon will present a screen telling you your limit is up.

Always Allowed

While you may want to cut down on some usage, you may deem other apps essential. Skype, for example, is classified in the social networking category, but you may need it for work. In Settings > Screen Time > Always Allowed you'll be able to set exceptions for apps you always need to access.

APPLE PAY

Apple Pay is now fully functional with all major banks in the US, UK and in many places throughout Asia and Europe. It lets you to use your phone the same way you'd use a contactless card.

How Does Apple Pay Work?

The iPhone features a Near Field Communications (NFC) chip that allows your phone to communicate with a contactless payment reader in a store. Once it has your card details it can send a one-time payment token to the retailer, rather than the card number. In that way it is considered more secure.

Setting Up Apple Pay

Apple Pay supports all of the major banks and card providers. Head to Settings > Wallet & Apple Pay to add your card details. Select Add Card and position your card in the frame and let the camera capture the details. You'll need to add a little more information on the next screen before verifying your wish to use the card. This will usually involve a call to the bank, which you'll be prompted to do.

Using Apple Pay

Apple Pay is usually available but you can always ask the attendant if unsure. When the cashier rings you up just place your phone close to the reader (as you would with a contactless card). You'll need to verify the transaction. It's done in different ways, depending on whether your phone uses Touch ID or Face ID.

Above: Adding your card details to Apple Pay is made easier by this capture screen.

- **Face ID**: Double-click the side button and glance at iPhone X to authenticate with Face ID. You can use your passcode too. Hold the phone close to the reader until you see Done on the display.

- **Touch ID**: Rest the authenticated digit on Touch ID and hold the top of your iPhone within a few centimeters of the contactless reader until you see Done on the screen.

Using Apple Pay in Apps

As well as in physical stores, Apple Pay also allows you to carry out transactions within apps like Groupon, Etsy and Uber. This will save you the hassle of entering your card details every time. During checkout select Buy With Apple Pay and then authenticate the purchase.

Apple Pay Cash

Apple Pay Cash is like your personal digital debit card. It enables you to send and receive cash within the Messages app (perhaps for splitting a dinner bill?), and also make Apple Pay payments with a balance. Here's how to set it up:

1. Tap Settings > Wallet & Apple Pay.

2. Turn on Apple Pay Cash and tap it under Payment Cards and follow the on screen instructions.

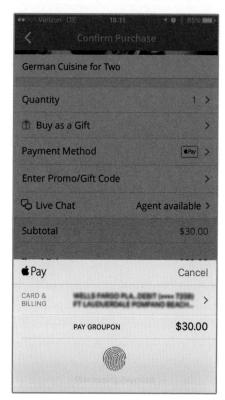

Above: You can pay for in-app purchases as well as transactions in shops with Apple Pay.

Hot Tip

If you have more than one card you can choose which to use. Hold the phone near the reader. You'll see the other options below your current card. Tap one to alter the payment method.

GET APPS

Although the iPhone has some excellent apps as standard, you'll definitely want to add your own, this is where the App Store comes in handy. You can buy and download apps on the move, from anywhere in the world.

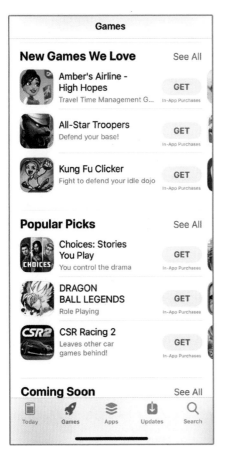

Apple ID

The App Store is another place where your Apple ID comes in handy. It allows you to download and purchase new content, while the password will also protect you from unauthorized downloads. We set up the Apple ID when setting up the phone, so your account should be ready to go when it comes to downloading apps.

Find Apps

Just like restaurants, bars or cafés, finding great new apps can be a real buzz. The main way to find out what's new and popular is by opening the App Store on your phone. Alternatively, just search the web or turn to page 250 for our guide to the Top 100 apps first.

Left: The App Store is where you'll find thousands of brilliant apps.

APP STORE

Apple recently redesigned the App Store to give it more of a magazine feel, suggesting apps for you to download in a variety of different categories. You'll see five tabs along the bottom of the screen: Today, Games, Apps, Updates and Search. Each represents a different way to discover new content.

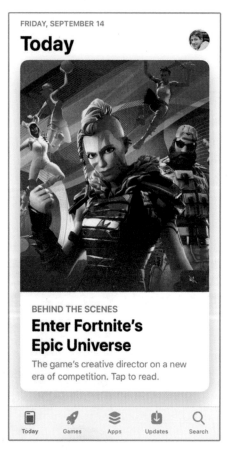

Above: The Today tab is a good place to start if you're looking to sample some new and trending apps for your phone.

Choose Your Apps

Once you've tapped the App Store icon on your Home screen to launch it, you'll see five tabs along the bottom of the screen:

- **Today:** An editorialised collection of featured apps from Apple. You may see categories like 'listen to the news' or 'bike to work'.

- **Games:** Here you'll see new and featured games, a number of collections, some recommendations from Apple, the top charts for games and a deeper dive into different gaming categories.

- **Apps:** Like the games section but for general app categories like Photo & Video, Health & Fitness, Shopping and Productivity. 'Featured' suggestions can be found at the top.

- **Updates:** Here you'll see available updates to your app library. If you have Automatic Updates switched on in Settings > iTunes & App Stores, you'll see the recently updated apps.

- **Search**: If you know the name of the app, you can type it into the search bar. Trending searches are shown in blue.

APP STORE PAGE

Once you've established the app you wish to download, you'll be taken to the product page. Here, you'll see the price or the word Get. If you already own it you'll see Open or Update (if one is available). There's also a star rating, which gives you an idea of how well it has been received. Below this information you'll see:

- **Details**: This offers screenshots, a description, what's new in the latest update and information on the size of the download, who makes it and which devices it supports.

- **Ratings and Reviews**: Read reviews from fellow iPhone users and write one of your own.

- **What's new**: Features/fixes in the latest update.

DOWNLOADING AN APP

Once you're convinced you want to download the app, tap the buy/install/get button. You may be asked to input your Apple ID password, but you can choose to authenticate the purchase with Touch ID or Face ID. Once that's been accepted, the app will

Hot Tip

If an app has a companion that works in Messages (*see* page 93) it'll be mentioned in the description.

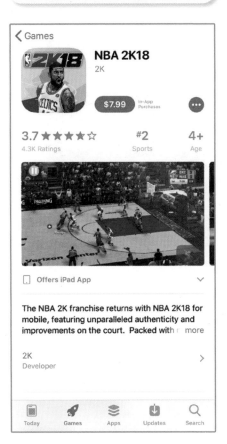

Above: The App Store product page offers all the information you need before downloading an app.

download. An app icon will appear on your Home screen, which says 'Loading'. Once it is installed, you'll be able open the app and use it.

Paid Apps and In-app Purchases

There are three main types of apps: free apps like Facebook, paid apps like Minecraft and 'Freemium' apps like Clash of Clans, which are free to download but require in-app purchases to play. The App Store page will tell you if an app offers in-app purchases.

Apple now requests authentication on in-app purchases. Pay for them by entering your Apple ID password or Touch ID or Face ID. In iOS 12, to lock down in-app purchases go to Settings > Screen Time > Content & Privacy Restrictions > iTunes & App Store Purchases and turn In-App Purchases to 'Don't Allow'.

ORGANIZE APPS

You can have multiple Home screens on your iPhone and each screen can hold up to 24 apps or folders.

Moving Apps

Press and hold any app icon until the apps begin to wiggle. You can now move any of them on the screen: just press an icon and drag it to a new location or into a folder. You can move it to another Home screen by dragging it to the far left or far right of the screen.

Create Folders

Above: Placing similar apps in folders saves space on your Home screen and lets you access similar apps quickly.

Creating folders is simple: press and hold any app on your Home screen until all the apps start to wiggle, then press

and drag the app you wish to drop into a folder on top of another app you also wish to have in that folder. Give the folder a name and you're good to go. To remove an app from a folder, just repeat the process and drag it back out.

Multitasking: Switching Between Apps

Rather than returning to the Home screen, finding the app and opening it, it's easy to switch between apps (*see* page 34).

Web Clips

In addition to stuffing your Home screens full of apps, you can also add shortcuts to your favourite websites so that there's no need to open Safari. In order to do this, just open the site in Safari and click the + button, followed by Add to Home Screen.

SIRI IN THIRD-PARTY APPS

Here's a few things you can do if you have the app in question installed on your phone:

- ◖ 'Siri, book me an Uber.' Get yourself a ride with Uber.

- ◖ 'Hey Siri, what song is this?' Shazam will tell you what song is playing.

- ◖ 'Siri, send cash to Brian.' Send money to your friends with PayPal.

Above: Siri works with third-party apps like Uber.

UPDATING APPS

App developers will issue updates of their apps in response to feedback they receive via iTunes or to release general improvements.

GET THE LATEST

If app updates are available, a badge will appear above the App Store icon on your Home screen. Within the Updates tab in the App Store app, an Update button will appear next to the app that needs refreshing. You can either press that or hit the Update All button to do them all at once. Alternatively head to Settings > iTunes & App Stores and turn on Updates in the Automatic Downloads menu.

Remove Apps

You can delete apps from your iPhone by holding down an icon until they begin to wiggle, then you can select the cross on the top left of the icon and you'll be asked to confirm you want to remove it from your phone. Press

Left: All updates can be performed at the same time within the App Store.

Done in the top left or the Home button to return to normal activity.

Share Apps

Sharing apps between your iOS devices will be taken care of automatically, provided you're syncing with iCloud. Head to Settings > iTunes & App Stores and enable Automatic Downloads for apps. This will ensure all devices using the Apple ID will automatically have that app installed.

App Settings and Preferences

The apps that come with the iPhone and the ones you download from the App Store have settings and preferences that you can edit. Every app will have its own functions available for customization, and there are two ways to tweak them:

○ **In Settings**: Go to Settings and scroll down the page until you see a list of apps. Not all apps will appear here, but those with settings to change will. Tap the app name to take a look at what can be customized.

○ **In the app**: Look for the words Options or Settings, or alternatively, an icon that looks like a cog. Failing that, there may be settings hiding within a More menu.

Above: You can delete apps by pressing down a finger on the Home screen (lightly on 3D Touch phones) and tapping the relevant cross.

Hot Tip

You can now delete most of the in-built apps Apple ships with the iPhone. So you can finally get rid of that Stocks app.

MULTIMEDIA

CAMERA

Your iPhone is a pretty nifty compact camera too. After reading the next few pages, you'll be convinced that you can leave your clunky compact at home.

Above: You can access the Camera app from your lock screen by swiping left once. On 3D Touch enabled devices you can press the icon in the bottom right corner.

STILLS CAMERA

There are few better smartphone cameras than on the latest iPhones. It will allow you to take pictures good enough to blow up and place on your mantelpiece with pride.

Taking Pictures

Once you have selected the Camera icon on the Home screen, you'll see the world in front of you on the iPhone's screen. This means that you're ready to start taking pictures, with one touch of the onscreen, in-app camera button. Simply touch it once to capture the image in a fraction of a second.

Taking Pictures With Volume Buttons

The iPhone has never had a physical camera button but you can use the volume keys as a shutter trigger, rather than the touch screen. It can make it much easier to hold the camera steady, rather than straining to reach the onscreen button, especially on the larger iPhones.

Taking Photos Faster

Photographs capture a fleeting, never-to-be-repeated moment, but by the time you've unlocked the phone with Face ID or Touch ID and then opened the Camera app – that moment may have passed. Apple realised this and created easy access to the Camera app from the lock screen. You can swipe left to open the Camera app directly from the lock screen – you'll be able to view the photos you take, but will have to unlock the phone to access the rest of your camera roll.

Focusing in on Your Subjects

When you open the iPhone Camera app, the sensor will seek to focus automatically on the item in the center of the frame and to give you a nicely balanced photo. It's wise to give the camera a second or so to complete this task before taking the photo.

Changing the Focus

Beyond autofocus, you can also tap anywhere on the screen to choose the precise area of the frame on which the sensor will focus. This is called tap-to-focus. Tapping this will define a smaller focus area, which comes in handy if you'd prefer to concentrate on a specific item within the frame or even something in the background.

Changing the Exposure

You should see a little sun icon next to the focus square, which indicates brightness. Drag this up and down to adjust the scene lighting. This will allow you to brighten up shots taken in lower light, but beware of altering the exposure too much, as it can look odd and will affect the quality of the photo.

Above: You can tap anywhere on the screen to bring up a yellow outline and make that area the focus of your photo.

Hot Tip
Select Take Portrait from the Camera app's 3D Touch options, to load the Portrait Mode.

Above: The yellow box indicates face detection.

Hot Tip

Rather than maxing out the zoom and ending up with out-of-focus photos, it's better to be cautious with the zooming.

Face Detection

Naturally, you'll be taking pictures of friends and family. When the iPhone spots faces in a picture, it will outline them with a yellow box, giving it extra focus.

Getting Closer to Your Subjects

On most cameras, there are dedicated buttons for zooming in and out, but this isn't the case with the iPhone, where any zooming needs to be done onscreen. In the same way you'd zoom in and out on a web page, use your thumb and forefinger to pinch in and out. This will also bring up a scroll bar at the foot of the screen. On iPhones with two rear cameras (iPhone 7 Plus/8 Plus/X/Xs/Xs Max) you can benefit from a telephoto lens.

Using the Flash

The camera on newer iPhone models is very effective in low-light conditions and will produce better pictures than you'd expect. However, there are times when using the flash is unavoidable. You'll see an icon in the top-left corner which says Auto, meaning that the iPhone will employ the flash at its discretion. You can tap this to override and turn the flash on or off.

Taking 'Selfies'

While some of the purpose of the front-facing camera is for video chat (see page 79), it's also great for self-portraits and group shots when the photographer is also in the frame. Touch the flip-camera icon in the bottom-right corner of the screen and take a photo as normal.

What's in a Megapixel?

Megapixels aren't as important as they used to be. These days it's more about the sensor's focal length, optical zoom and aperture capabilities. However, the newest iPhones have 12-megapixel, rear-facing, wide-angle and telephoto lenses. The front-facing camera is 7 megapixels.

OTHER PHOTO OPTIONS

Apple has spent a lot of time improving the camera options on the iPhone, and there are now quite a few tricks at iPhone users' disposal. The various shooting options are displayed in a carousel beneath the frame. You can move between them by swiping left and right anywhere on the shooting screen. The default, of course, is photo.

Below: You can swipe over to the 'Square' shooting mode to frame your photo differently.

Above: The iPhone camera options allow you to choose between photo and video settings, add filters, view previous photos and more.

Square

Another photo mode is Square (swipe to the right). This changes the aspect ratio of the photo to, you guessed it, a square. This is handy if you intend to upload the photo to Instagram, which uses a Polaroid-style square framing.

Portrait Mode (Dual Lens iPhones Only)

The Portrait Mode uses both of the rear-facing iPhone cameras in tandem to create a cool 'bokeh' effect. This focuses on the subject while blurring the background, giving you crisp portraits with a great depth effect. Below the frame you'll see a carousel of shooting options. Swipe to the right to highlight Portrait.

Above: The Portrait mode on newer iPhones allows you to take vivid photos with a neat depth effect that blurs the background.

1. Line up your subject. You may receive a message asking you to move closer or further away.

2. When you hit the sweet spot, you'll see a yellow indicator. On the iPhone X and up, you'll also see Portrait Lighting options like Natural Light and Studio Light, which you can flick between.

3. You'll see the depth effect and lighting options (where available) in real time, allowing you to see how the final shot will look. Hit the shutter whenever you're ready.

Panoramas (Pano)

You can capture a sweeping landscape or a big family photo with the Pano setting. This requires little more than a steady hand. Select the Pano option to begin.

1. Position the phone at the left edge of where you'd like the panorama to begin and press the camera trigger button. The first shot will appear.

2. As steadily as possible, pan the camera to the right, trying to keep the arrow in the center of the spirit level-type indicator. The progress of the scene will be depicted in the indicator.

3. When you're done, hit Capture again and tap the thumbnail to view the results.

High Dynamic Range

Switching on HDR can offer much better photos. In simple terms, it takes a photo at three exposure settings – Underexposed, Overexposed and Normal – and combines the best elements of all three. From the iPhone 8 and up, it's used automatically.

Timer

The iPhone camera has a timer option at the top of the display. Tapping this will allow you to set a 10-second interval before the photo is taken to get yourself ready.

Live Photos

Live Photos (iPhone 6s and up) are awesome. These capture 1.5 seconds of video and audio before and after the photo on both cameras. So, for example, instead of just getting the still portrait, you have the person getting into position and saying cheese. It's a lovely feature and here's how it works:

1. Make sure you line up the photo first. The live photos icon is represented by a bullseye in the top center of the camera interface. Tap this to enable Live Photos.

2. Take the photo as you normally would and keep the camera in place. The phone will record another second and a half of video (indicated by the word live in yellow).

Photo Filters

The iPhone now offers a select number of live photo filters that allow you to change the appearance of your photo

Above: Live Photos are a great way to capture moments with a few seconds of video before and after a photo.

Hot Tip

Hold down on the shutter button for 'burst' photos. You can then select the best from the camera roll and discard the rest.

before you take it. Tapping the filters icon in the top right corner of the screen (bottom right in earlier versions) shows a grid of thumbnails, showing the different filter options to choose from.

Switching Between Lenses

There are two 12-megapixel lenses on the back of the iPhone (from the iPhone 7/7 Plus and up). Lens one is wide-angled with focal length of f/1.8 and will allow you to get a little more into the frame. The second lens, is a 'telephoto' one with a focal length of f/2.8. This enables you to get closer to subjects and offers a 2x optical zoom, which means you won't lose any clarity. It's simple to switch between the lenses on newer iPhones. Just above the shutter there's a 1x icon. Tapping this will make that x2 and signify the switch to the second telephoto lens.

RECORDING VIDEO

Any smartphone worth its salt is now capable of recording high definition video, heck the newer iPhones can even shoot video at the new 4K standard matching what's on offer from dedicated camcorders. There is no dedicated app for the iPhone's video camera; instead, it's easily accessible from inside the Camera app. Swipe one step right from Photo and you'll switch to Video mode. Tap the red button to begin/end. If you have two rear cameras on your iPhone, you can easily switch between them for video zooming too by tapping the x1/x2 button.

Take Stills While Recording Video

Even if you're shooting video of a gleeful youngster blowing out his birthday candles, the camera is capable of performing double duty by capturing

Left: The iPhone can shoot HD or 4K video, depending on your model. You can also shoot stills using the white button.

still shots. After pressing the Record button, you'll see the camera icon next to it – press this to save a still shot. Best of all, the shutter won't make its usual clicking sound and disturb your video.

Slow-motion Video

You can also use your iPhone's video camera (5s and up) to shoot in slow motion. A normal speed video as captured at 30 frames per second, but the best iPhones can shoot slow motion video at up to 240 frames per second, while preserving HD (1080p) resolution. This looks great when capturing action videos.

Shooting in Slo-Mo Mode

Swipe over to Slo-mo then simply hit the Capture button and record as normal until you've captured your footage. Then select the thumbnail icon to play it back. You can adjust the sliders to determine which elements of the clip appear in slo-mo. In order to change the frame rate, go to Settings > Camera > Record Slo-mo.

Above: Record timelapse videos to condense a few minutes of action into a few seconds of video. Great for sunsets!

Timelapse Mode

Timelapse mode effectively takes a still photo at 'dynamically selected intervals', then stitches the results together in a video. The result enables you to see action captured over a number of minutes condensed into a few seconds. This works great for capturing a sunrise or sunset or perhaps a bike ride or car journey.

STORING AND VIEWING PHOTOS AND VIDEOS

Once you have taken lots of lovely photos and captured precious moments on video, you will want to make sure they are stored away safely.

CAMERA ROLL

After you've taken a photo or recorded a video, it'll leap into thumbnail icon in the bottom-left corner. This is your Camera Roll, where all of your recordings are automatically stored on your iPhone's internal memory.

1. Press the thumbnail from within the photo capture screen to take you to the last shot. This is great if you're looking to share or edit a picture instantly. You can swipe left or right to move between shots.

2. Or select the Photos app from the Home screen to access a feed of pictures in the Photos tab, with the newest at the bottom. Here you'll also see the tabs For You, Albums and Search. All of them allow you to find photos and begin interacting with them.

For You and Albums in Photos

The For You tab features content intelligently curated. It automatically sorts groups of photos into albums.

Left: The Photos section of the app splits images into location-based Collections. Click on a thumbnail to edit or share.

These could be based on dates like 'last weekend' or places, like 'UK 2014' or the people you're with called 'together.' While the Albums tab features a combination of albums you've created, have been shared with you, and photos you've earmarked as a favourite. You'll also be able to see albums called People & Places. This intelligent assistant recognises the faces in your photos and uses geo-tagging to assign locations to those pictures.

Backing Up Photos

Your precious memories are safeguarded whenever you back up your iPhone: physically via iTunes or over the web via iCloud. Remember to back up all of your photos via iCloud, you'll probably need a storage plan (see page 43 for iCloud backup instructions). Alternatively, there are lots of apps that do this, including Google Photos with unlimited free storage.

Creating Photo Albums on Your iPhone

1. Select the Photos app, select Albums and hit the + button in the top-left corner. Select New Album. Name the album and you'll be taken to the Photos screen, which separates images by the dates and locations.

2. Tap the thumbnails to add blue ticks next to each photo and press Done when you've finished. A new album will appear in the Photos app under the Albums tab.

3. To add more photos to any album, enter the album, tap Select > Add choose more photos. You can also select an individual photo, hit the Share button and select Add to Album.

Step 2 (right): Select photos from your Camera Roll to add to an album.

Above: Straighten out wonky photos.

EDITING PHOTOS

Taking photos and recording video on the iPhone is just the start. They can be fine-tuned using a number of apps and then easily shared with friends and the world at large.

Editing Pictures Using the Photos App

The Photos app features a few built-in editing tools that allow you to fine-tune your photos before sharing or printing them. Select a picture from your Camera Roll or an album and select the levels indicator at the bottom of the screen. The options that appear are the following:

- **Auto Enhance:** Tap the magic wand in the top-right to magically adjust the lighting in your photo. It doesn't always work, but in many cases, it's a quick fix.

- **Crop:** Cut out unwanted elements by dragging the Crop tool in and out. Here, you can also straighten the photo and rotate it in increments of 90 degrees.

- **Filter:** The filters accessed by tapping the three circles can be added live or after the fact. Add a filter to give the photo a different look and feel.

- **Colour and Lighting:** Select Light, Color or B&W to adjust the intensity of the effect by sliding the dials.

- **Mark Up:** Here you can annotate photos by handwriting on them, adding text or, using the little magnifying glass to zoom in on parts of the image.

When you've completed the edits, press Done at the bottom or Cancel to return the photo to its original state.

More iPhone Editing Apps

The built-in photo-editing tools on the iPhone are very limited. However, there's a host of downloadable applications that offer much more flexibility when editing the look and feel of your photo before you share it. The likes of Camera+ and Photoshop Touch are great options to consider, while the photo-sharing network Instagram has a wealth of editing tools.

 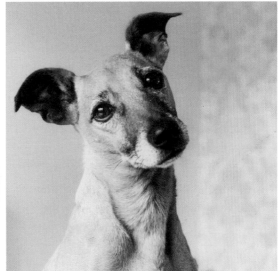

Above: Use the free Instagram app to take ordinary photos and give them a little extra flair through cropping and filters.

SHARING PHOTOS

Throughout the second and third chapters, we've explained how to share photos through email, Messages, Facebook and Twitter, via the Share icon that appears whenever you're viewing a photo in the Photos app. There are a few more options, however, that we have yet to encounter when you press the Share icon.

- **Use as Wallpaper**: You can easily set images from your Camera Roll as your background. Scale the photo and select Wallpaper, Lock Screen – or both.

- **Print**: If your iPhone is configured to work with a Wi-Fi printer, you can instantly print off a snap from your Photos app.

- **Assign to Contact**: Got a photo you'd like to see every time you get a call or email from a contact? Select this option and match it up with a contact.

- **Copy**: Tap this to paste the photo within another application, such as a third-party email app like Gmail that doesn't sit within the Share menu.

- **Airdrop**: If another iPhone is nearby and has Bluetooth enabled, you'll see it pop up in the Airdrop menu. Tap their contact icon to share.

Above: The Photo sharing screen presents you with options such as setting an image as your wallpaper.

Favourites

It's helpful to keep track of your choice snaps in an album of their own. Tapping the Heart icon beneath the photo within the camera roll will ensure it is added to a Favourites album.

iCLOUD PHOTO LIBRARY

This is slightly different to Photo Stream (*see right*). It allows you to automatically upload and store your entire library in iCloud and make it accessible on all of your iCloud-enabled devices. Enabling iCloud Photo Library (Settings > Your Name > iCloud) will use your free 5 GB of storage.

If you need more, you can purchase it from one of the monthly plans, which start at $0.99/79p a month for 50 GB.

MY PHOTO STREAM

Photo Stream is the part of iCloud that is responsible for syncing and backing up your photos. It is one of the very best reasons for enabling iCloud when you set up your device. If you enable Photo Stream (Settings > Your Name > iCloud > Upload to Photo Stream), every picture you take using your iPhone will be automatically uploaded to iCloud and viewable across a host of devices, such as an iPad or the Photos app on your Mac if you have one. This maxes out at 1,000 photos in 30 days. Once that limit is reached, older photos will be deleted. This, however, doesn't count towards your 5 GB iCloud storage.

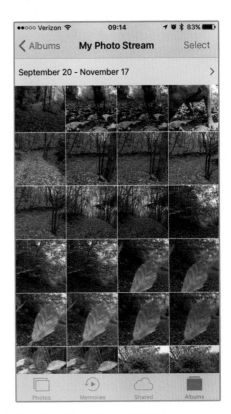

Sharing Camera Roll Photos to Photo Stream
Once Photo Stream is enabled, you don't have to do anything to upload a photo. It's all done automatically, provided your iPhone is connected to Wi-Fi (if you're not, the iPhone will still upload the pictures next time you are).

Viewing the Photo Stream
Within the Albums section of the Photos app, there is a tab for Photo Stream. All of the photos you've shared to Photo Stream from your various Apple devices (not just those taken using the iPhone) are visible and sharable from this tab.

Viewing Photos from Other Apple Devices
Photo Stream – and indeed iCloud in general – is most useful to people who have multiple Apple devices. For example, if you have a Mac computer, photographs you

Above: Photo Stream stores up to 1,000 photos for 30 days.

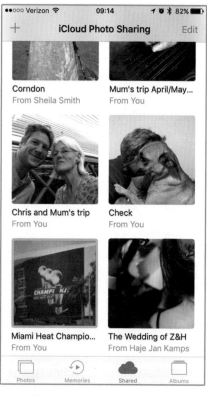

Above: iCloud Photo Sharing helps you share albums with friends and family.

import to the Photos program from your dedicated digital camera (Canon, Sony, etc.) can be automatically uploaded to Photo Stream (Photos > Preferences > Photo Stream > Automatic Upload) and will appear in your Photo Stream on the iPhone within seconds.

iCloud Photo Sharing

Although Photo Stream can be for personal use, you can also set up iCloud Photo Sharing to share photos and albums with others. Here's how to set up shared Photo Streams:

1. Go to Settings > Photos and switch on iCloud Photos. Go to the Photos app.

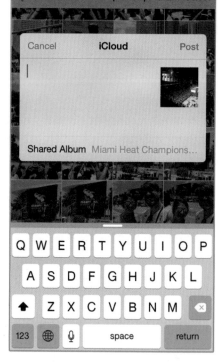

Step 3: You can add comments before you add a photo to an iCloud shared album.

2. Hit the Select button and tap the photos you'd like to share. Select the Share button and pick iCloud Photo Sharing.

3. A new sharing card will load with the photos attached. You can add a comment, select an existing shared album or create a new one.

4. Browse to the Shared tab in the Photos app and select your new album. Then tap People > Invite People. Choose a contact and they'll be notified via email.

5. Choose whether subscribers can post as well. This is great if you would like the invited parties to share photos within this album too.

Family Albums

If you have Family Sharing set up, it'll automatically create an album within the Shared section of the Photos app. You can share pictures to this using the methods explained above.

EDITING AND SHARING VIDEOS

Videos shot on your iPhone can also be tweaked and sent out to the rest of the world – or just your mum.

Trim Video Recordings

The Trim tool dispenses with the unwanted portions of a video, making the clip nicer to look at and easier to share (due to the reduced file size).

Above: Edit video recordings using the Trim tool.

1. Select the video clip from the Camera Roll. There are markers at the beginning and end of each video. Drag the markers to where you'd like the clip to start and end.

Below: You can choose whether to publish a video to YouTube in Standard Definition or HD.

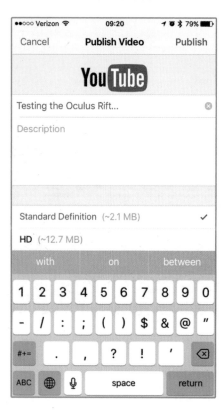

2. The video timeline bar will turn yellow and a new Trim button will appear.

3. Once the clip is tailored to your satisfaction, press the Play button to preview the new edit.

4. Once you're happy, press Trim. You'll be asked whether you'd like to Trim Original or Save As New Clip; the latter will keep both versions. The new clip will then be ready to share.

Sharing Videos via Facebook, Email and Messages

To share a video, select the clip from the Camera Roll and hit the Share icon. You can select from the usual options. Select Email or Messages to load the video in a blank email or message, add the contact details and accompanying text, and press Send.

Publish Videos to YouTube

It doesn't appear within the native Share video for newer versions of iOS, but you can also upload the video to YouTube, giving it a much larger potential audience. Here's how to do it:

1. Download the YouTube app from the App Store.

2. Open the YouTube app and sign into your account (it's your Gmail account details, if you have one). Tap the camcorder icon at the top of the display. Select a pre-

shot video from the list below (you can also record directly from the app or choose to broadcast live).

3. Trim the video, add effects and music and hit Next.

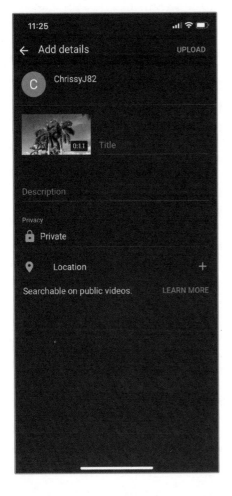

4. Type a title and description for the video in the respective fields.

5. Tap the globe icon to make the video Public, Unlisted (available only to people with whom you share the link) or Private (only people you invite can view it). Tap the pin icon to choose whether the video location is included.

6. Select Publish to upload the video.

Left: You can upload a video to the web using the YouTube app.

MUSIC

The iPhone itself rose from the success of Apple's iPod. Hands up if you've owned an iPod? OK, everyone put your hands down now. The iPod is now dead, but thankfully the iPhone is a great music player in its own right. It has great audio quality, a music store and Apple Music.

GETTING MUSIC ON YOUR iPHONE

There are three major ways to approach this. You can transfer your own music onto the phone via iTunes, or buy it from the iTunes Music Store. However, recent trends have shifted towards streaming services like Apple Music. We'll outline these options on the next pages.

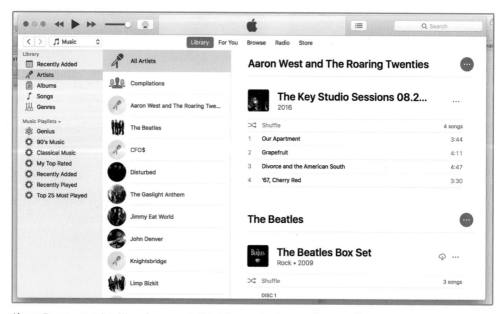

Above: iTunes is a great digital library for your music. Select albums and tracks to transfer to your iPhone.

SYNCING VIA iTUNES

If you have a big digital music collection on your computer, from imported CDs for example, you can transfer the music to your iPhone via the iTunes program. Next time you sync the iPhone via iTunes on your computer (see page 41):

1. Open the iPhone menu and tap Music on the sidebar.

2. Tick Sync Music and choose whether you want your entire library or just selected artists and playlists. If you have a big library it will fill your hard drive quite quickly.

3. Tap Sync at the bottom of the screen when done and you music will begin transferring.

THE iTUNES MUSIC STORE

The emergence of streaming platforms like Apple Music have meant purchases of digital music are down, but you can still buy albums and songs from the iTunes Store app. From the contemporary to the classic, it's all there waiting for you under one roof.

Buying Music on the iTunes Store

1. Tap the app to go online to the iTunes store and select Music at the bottom.

2. If there's a particular type of music you like – from Pop to Hip Hop – select it using the Genres button at the top of the screen.

3. Scroll down the page and you can see lots of different

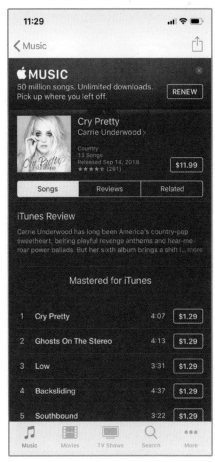

Step 6: Buy a track by tapping the price button to its right, then the buy button. To buy the whole album, tap the price button at the top of the page.

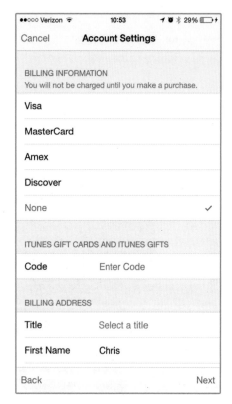

Cancel   **Account Settings**

BILLING INFORMATION
You will not be charged until you make a purchase.

Visa

MasterCard

Amex

Discover

None   ✓

ITUNES GIFT CARDS AND ITUNES GIFTS

Code   Enter Code

BILLING ADDRESS

Title   Select a title

First Name   Chris

Back   Next

Step 7: You may be asked to enter payment details for your Apple ID.

Hot Tip

If you have a large library and only want to sync certain artists to your iPhone, you can choose selected playlists, artists, albums and genres from the Sync music tab and apply each manually.

selections, such as new albums, themed collections, and what's hot. There are also recommendations just for you. If you know what you want, use the Search tab at the bottom.

4. Once you have selected an album or song, tap to go through to the information page. This includes details of the artist, the release date and average rating by other iTunes users, plus the price button. Underneath is a listing of the track(s).

5. Tap the song title to listen to a 90 second sample of the track.

6. To buy an individual track, tap the price button to the right and then the price button. If it's the album on which the track features that you want to buy, tap the price button at the top of the page.

7. You may be asked to enter your payment details, if this is the first time you are purchasing something.

8. If you have a big collection, you may and end up trying to buy a track you have already purchased. If this was bought in the iTunes store, Download appears instead of the price, so you won't be charged again.

9. While the items are being downloaded, tap the More button and then Downloads to see their progress.

APPLE MUSIC

People have moved away from buying digital music and towards streaming. For the price of one album a month you can get unlimited access to more than 45 million songs. With the Apple Music subscription service you'll also get unlimited radio, personalized and curated music lists, hand-selected by experts as well as your own music library saved for offline playback when you have no Wi-Fi.

It's a fantastic way to have all kinds of new and old music at your disposal. Tap For You in the Music app to choose your plan.

Cost and Cancelling

Apple Music costs £9.99/$9.99 a month, but you can cancel at any time via Settings > Your Name > iTunes & App Store > Apple ID > View Apple ID > Subscriptions. If you do this before the end of your (free) three month trial you won't be charged.

Getting Started with Apple Music

Once you've signed up you'll be asked to pick the categories you're into. Select Next to choose Artists. This will give you some Playlists to sample by swiping left and right. The idea is that as you listen the service learns more about your taste and you'll get better recommendations.

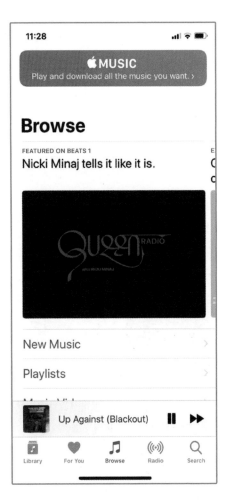

Above: Apple Music is a streaming service that puts hand-selected music, radio and your library, all in one place.

Finding Music in Apple Music

While the browse category can be handy for finding new music, you'll probably be more likely to search for specific artists depending on what you want to listen to. Searching for music is just the same as in the iTunes Store, only this time you don't have to open your wallet again.

Adding Music to Your Library

When you've found what you want you can play it as you see fit. But for faster access you can add it to your Library, where it'll sit alongside your purchased or transferred music. You can Tap the + icon to add anything to your Library, which is the first tab at the bottom of the screen.

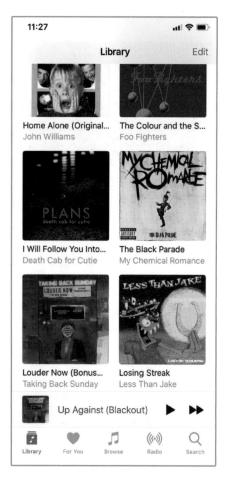

Other Music Streaming Services

Apple offers a fantastic solution in Apple Music, but it wasn't the first and isn't the most popular. That's Spotify. Google Play Music and Amazon Prime Music Unlimited are also popular.

THE MUSIC APP

This is the place to play much of your music content. It can store your digital music library from iTunes, purchased music from the iTunes Store and streamed albums and songs from the Apple Music service.

Play Music

1. Tap the Music icon to open it. In the splash screen that opens you'll have the choice to Join Apple Music, Apple's streaming service. If you want to give Apple Music a shot, you get a free month no-risk trial. If not, select Not Now.

2. This takes you to your Library where you'll see your music, with Playlists, Artists, Albums and Songs above

Left: Apple Music features your library, suggestions 'For You' and content from artists that you follow.

a selection of Recently Added songs. Here you'll see any music purchased from iTunes, music synced from your computer's music library and Apple Music tracks you've purposely saved to your library.

3. Select the artist, album or tile of the song you want and then tap the song to begin playback. For albums you'll also see options to shuffle the tunes.

4. The Now Playing screen sits at the bottom of the screen. You can access basic controls from here, such as play, pause and skip to the next track.

5. You can tap or swipe up from the Now Playing screen to see more controls.

6. Here you'll see album art, song titles, a playhead scrubber, the volume slider, the skip track buttons and the opportunity to send the audio to different speakers (the red triangle with the spiral above).

7. Tap More to download the song (if it's stored in iTunes or Apple Music), delete it from the library, add it to a playlist, or share it with another user (perhaps via iMessage?). Tapping the Love or Dislike hearts will help Apple Music generate recommendations in the For You section (applies to Apple Music subscribers only).

Above: The iPhone music player displays the controls. Seen here the scrubber bar, the volume slider, and the download icon (the cloud with an arrow).

The Music Queue

Hidden beneath the Now Playing screen is the queue of songs you've got on tap (just swipe slowly up). This is called Up Next. If you're playing an album, you'll see the remaining tracks in the list. Here you'll also see the Shuffle and Repeat options.

Hot Tip

Press down (like you would for 3D touch) the mini player in the Control Center for an expanded view of the controls, and the ability to change the audio output source.

- **To add a song**: From anywhere in the Music app you can add a song to the queue. Tap the three dots menu next to the track (or use 3D Touch) and tap Play Next or Play Later to add it to the end of the current queue.

- **To rearrange the queue**: Tap the three lines next to the track and move them up and down the list.

- **To remove a song**: Swipe the track name from right to left.

Saving Apple Music Offline

If you do take the plunge with Apple Music you're going to want to save your albums and songs offline so you can play them when you're away from an internet connection (or, at the very least, to save precious data). Here's how:

- Before you save your content offline

you must first add it to your Library by tapping
the + icon.

- To download it to your iPhone tap the iCloud icon
  from the relevant section of your library.

- You'll see a tick and the word 'downloaded'
  when complete.

- You can also turn Automatic Downloads on to ensure
  anything you add to your library is automatically
  downloaded to the device (over Wi-Fi). Go to Tap
  Settings > Your Name > iTunes & App Store and toggle
  Music to On.

Multitasking with Music

The great thing about the Music app is you don't have to
keep it open. You can find the music you want and then
leave the app. It'll continue playing unless you attempt to
play media in another app. If music is playing you'll see a
mini player, on the lock screen and in the Control Center.

Searching Your Songs

Rather than scroll through one long list, you can locate a
particular song you want by tapping the magnifying glass icon and typing in the Search box.
Select the appropriate tab to search Apple Music or your library.

Creating Playlists

1. Tap Library > Playlists and you'll see any existing playlists. To start a new one, tap the
   New Playlist button.

Above: You can quickly access music
controls from the Control Center.

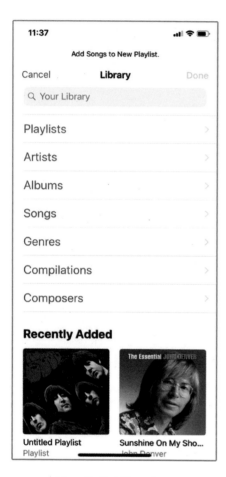

Q Your Library

Playlists   >

Artists   >

Albums   >

Songs   >

Genres   >

Compilations   >

Composers   >

Recently Added

The Essential JOHN DENVER

Untitled Playlist
Playlist

Sunshine On My Sho...
John Denver

Above: Tap the Add songs button to start selecting music by Artists, Albums etc., that you want to include on your playlist.

2. In the box that opens give the playlist a name that readily describes its content and tap the camera icon to add an image.

3. Tap the Add Music button. Here you can select from music folders in your library (artists, albums, etc.) or use the search bar to find specifics.

4. The list of Songs on your iPhone opens. Tap the + button beside those you want to add to the playlist. When you have added all the songs you would like to your playlist, just tap the Done button.

5. Playlists can be edited easily by tapping a playlist from the list and selecting edit. Here you can tap the green + to add more music or the red – to delete tracks. You can also rearrange songs by pressing and holding the three lines icon and dragging it up and down.

Find Playlists

Making the perfect playlist is a labour of love, but sometimes you just want to dive right in. If you subscribe to Apple Music you get access to a host of playlists created just for you, based on your listening habits and previously expressed interests. You'll see these, naturally, in the For You section.

Radio

If you have Apple Music, you can always use the Music app to listen to customizable radio stations. Tap Radio and search for Radio Stations. You can also search for any song, hold down your finger on the screen and select 'Create Station' for a playlist based on songs and artists.

PODCASTS

There are thousands of hours of podcasts – audio and video shows – on a stunning range of topics that cover virtually everything from self-help, comedy, true crime, to sports and business. Time to tune in.

Finding Podcasts

Apple's free Podcast app is built in to iOS. When you open the app, it will show your Listen Now screen with podcasts you've already subscribed to and shows you might like.

1. Tap the Library tab to see your own shows, episodes and downloaded episodes.

2. To see all the available podcasts, tap the Browse button at the bottom of the screen.

3. If you're seeking something in particular, tap Search. This will also show trending searches.

4. Once you've identified a show, tap the thumbnail for full details of the available episodes, how long they are, together with other users' ratings and reviews.

5. Tap on the title of a single episode to begin playing it, or press the + button later consumption. 3D Touch is helpful here too.

6. Alternatively, you can press the Subscribe button from the main podcast page, and the latest episode will be downloaded. You will also get future episodes downloaded automatically as they become available.

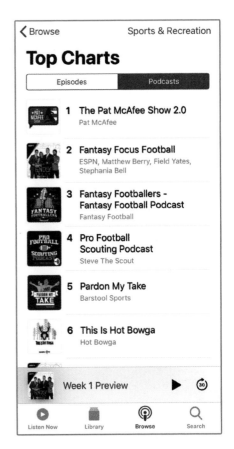

Above: Browse popular podcasts within a category by swiping through the options.

Above: Apple AirPods use
W1 technology to sync with
the iPhone.

HEADPHONES AND SPEAKERS

If you're at home, you can play music through the iPhone's speakers;
they're actually not bad! If you're in public, you'll need some wired
or wireless headphones. However, if you're looking to crank up the
volume, you can have your music super loud with the aid of a speaker.

The Headphones Conundrum

Every iPhone before the iPhone 7 and 7 Plus featured a standard
3.5mm headphone jack. The new models ditched it so in the iPhone
box you'll see an adapter that plugs into the charging port that you
can use to connect traditional wired headphones, including the
bundled EarPods. This works fine, except when you need to charge
the phone too.

Wireless Headphones

You can connect any Bluetooth headphones to the iPhone and Apple
has wireless AirPods (*see* page 18). They aren't cheap but reviews are
good. You can find out more at Apple.com/airpods.

Speaker Docks

Speaker docks allow you to plug your iPhone into a more powerful set of speakers.
Some are great, because they'll also charge your iPhone while it is docked.

AirPlay Speakers

AirPlay is a wireless technology developed by Apple to share music and video over Wi-Fi
networks. If you have AirPlay-enabled speakers (they're available from Bose, Sony, JBL and
more), you can send any music from your iPhone to the speakers without plugging in.
If an AirPlay speaker is connected to the same Wi-Fi network as your iPhone, you'll see the
AirPlay icon (a triangle with three circles). Look for it in the Music app and in the Control
Center. Tap the icon and select your speaker of choice.

Bluetooth with Headphones and Speakers

You can also use Bluetooth connectivity to connect to speakers and headphones – here's how:

Hot Tip

If you own an Apple TV, you can send music directly to your TV set.

1. Make sure that Bluetooth is enabled on the device.

2. Enter the iPhone Settings and select Bluetooth. Toggle the switch to turn Bluetooth on.

3. The iPhone will go into Discovery mode and search for speakers with Bluetooth connectivity.

4. When you find your Bluetooth device (usually under the manufacturer's name and model number), select it.

5. You may be asked for a four-digit PIN code to connect (see your instructions). Once the initial connection is made, it will connect automatically in future.

6. Enter the Music app (or Spotify or internet radio apps, etc.) and start playing.

Above: These are Libratone Zipp bluetooth speakers that are compatible with AirPlay.

Wired Speakers

You can also connect speakers through the iPhone's headphone jack on older models, but you'll need an adapter on iPhones without the 3.5mm port.

VIDEO

The iPhone is a staggeringly powerful tool for video. Not only can it record video at resolutions up to 4K, you can also play your favourite TV shows and movies, stream them from the internet and purchase brand new films to rent and own.

ADDING VIDEO CONTENT TO YOUR iPHONE

If you read the section in this chapter on syncing your music files, then you'll soon notice that the process of getting video content on to your phone is pretty similar. It can be bought or streamed directly from the internet, or added from your existing library.

Above: Sync your favourite TV shows over iTunes so that you can watch them on your iPhone.

Syncing Video via iTunes

Just as we did with music, it's possible to transfer existing videos you may have previously purchased or added to iTunes directly on to your iPhone. Remember, anything you've previously purchased from iTunes will be available in the Video app thanks to iCloud.

1. Plug your iPhone into your computer using the USB cable; iTunes should automatically load (if you don't have iTunes, *see* page 187). Then select the iPhone from the navigation menu.

2. From the content menu on the left-hand side, select Movies or TV Shows. You'll see a list of videos you currently have within your iTunes library.

3. Tick Sync Music or Movies/TV Shows and then select the content you'd like to add.

4. Alternatively, tick the Automatically Include box and select from the drop-down menu to set rules (all movies, most recent, unwatched, etc).

5. The Capacity bar at the bottom of the iTunes screen will tell you how much space you have on the device and will update as you add video files.

6. When you're done, press Sync and the movies or TV shows will begin to load on to your device. Don't unplug the iPhone until this process is complete.

iPhone/iTunes Video Formats

Apple likes to keep things tidy, but it also likes you to buy things from them. To that end, it limits the video formats that work in iTunes and on the iPhone. The files need to be .MPEG-4 or .H.264 to play on the device. Videos in other popular formats, such as .WMV and .AVI, will not work on the iPhone or in iTunes.

Hot Tip

It is possible to watch videos in formats not recognized by Apple, such as .WMV or .AVI; they can be converted on your computer using software such as Handbreak (www. handbreak.com).

BUYING FROM THE iTUNES STORE

You can purchase a world of movie and TV content through the iTunes app on your iPhone. Whatever you buy will be synced across all devices associated with your Apple ID.

Finding Video Content

Open the iTunes app and select the Movies or TV Shows tab to see featured content. This will show new releases and recently aired shows. In order to locate content, hit the Search button and type in the title of your choice.

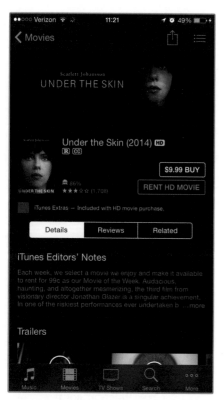

Above: The video product page gives added info about movies or TV shows featured on iTunes.

The Video Product Page

Once you've found the movie of your choice, you'll be taken to its product page, where you'll have the opportunity to view trailers. You'll also see a plot summary, cast and crew list, and a certificate, and you'll get the chance to read reviews from other users.

Buying to Own

Buying video content from the iTunes app means that the digital file is yours to keep for ever. You can access it on as many Apple devices as you please and it will always be associated with your Apple ID.

1. Identify the movie or TV show you wish to own. Click the price button and enter your account password or authenticate with Touch ID. Once that's done, the file will start downloading.

2. You can see its progress by selecting More > Downloads within iTunes and it'll give you an indication of how long is left to download.

3. In order to start watching as the movie is downloading, exit iTunes and enter the TV app. It'll be waiting for you in the Library.

4. Select the title to begin playback.

Renting Movies

iTunes movie rentals are perfect if you just want to watch a movie once rather than have it to own. The price is around the same as renting a DVD from your local video store (remember those?). In iTunes, you follow the same procedure as buying a movie (unfortunately, TV shows can only be bought to own), except that you hit the Rent button from the product page.

There are a couple of caveats with renting movies though. Once you begin to watch the film, it has to be finished within 48 hours. Otherwise, you have 30 days before the rental expires. The TV app will tell you how long you have left to view the video.

HD or SD?

Prices for movies and TV shows are automatically displayed for the HD version but, if you're not concerned about the highest quality, you get the video more cheaply by scrolling to the bottom of the product page screen and selecting Also Available in SD (Standard Definition).

Above: The TV app tells you how long you have left to view a rented iTunes movie.

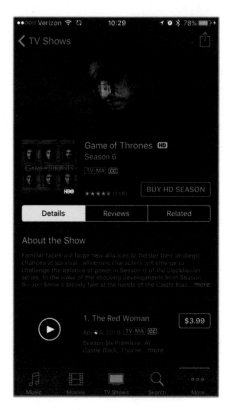

Above: For TV series, you can either buy a pass to view the whole season or scroll down to select a certain episode.

Season Pass or Episodes?

If you're buying TV shows from iTunes, you'll have the option to pick up the latest episode or to buy a pass, which gives you the entire season. The first option is great if you have a favourite episode or you missed one when it was aired on TV. The season home page will point you towards buying the whole season, but scroll down the page to access particular episodes.

Downloading Your Movies

Since movie and TV show files are so large, you may not be able to fit multiple films on the iPhone at one time – especially if you've only got the 16-GB model.

iTunes keeps a record of everything you've bought from the store (either from the iTunes computer app for Mac and PC, or on your iPhone or iPad) and lets you reacquire the content wirelessly. To re-download previous purchases, go to iTunes Store > More > Purchased and select the iCloud download button from the title page. The file will then be downloaded to your device.

Above: You can download previous movie purchases to your phone by connecting to Wi-Fi and using iCloud.

THE TV APP

Formerly known as Video (iOS 10 and earlier) the
iPhone's TV app houses all of the content you currently
have stored on the device, either transferred from iTunes
or bought/rented from iTunes. There's also a smart For
You tab that will introduce recommendations from other
apps you may have installed on your phone, like the BBC
iPlayer or ITV Player.

Playing Movies

The video playback screen
on the iPhone is a lot
simpler than the music
equivalent. Selecting a video
from the app will instantly
start playback.

iTunes Sharing
Over Wi-Fi

If your iPhone and
computer are connected to
the same mobile network,

Above: Playing movies in the Video app is simple. When you touch the screen, it will
display Play, Pause, Rewind and Forward buttons, along with a progress bar.

you can stream items from your iTunes library directly to your iPhone via iTunes Home
Sharing. Open the TV app and select Shared. Select your Library and all of the video files listed
on your computer will show up; you can then play them as normal.

AirPlay via Apple TV

When you're watching a movie on the train on the way home from work, wouldn't it be nice to
just send it to your television when you get through the door and relax in your favourite chair
to watch the ending? If you have an Apple TV set-top box, that's exactly what you can do.

We mentioned AirPlay in the Music section, but it extends to video for Apple TV owners too. Videos from an increasing number of apps and websites now have AirPlay support. Here's how to share video with your TV:

1. You'll need to be registered on the same Wi-Fi network as the Apple TV.

2. If it's in range, you'll see the AirPlay icon in the video playback controls. Tap this and select Apple TV.

3. The video will automatically be transferred at exactly the same point in your viewing.

Left and Below: Selecting the AirPlay icon in the Control Center allows you to use AirPlay to transfer content to your Apple TV at home.

VIDEO STREAMING SERVICES

Although Apple would love you to rent and buy videos only from the iTunes Store, there are plenty of other alternatives in the App Store for streaming video over the internet. Here are some of our favourites; see also a list of our favourite apps on page 251.

- **Amazon Prime Instant Video**: Subscribers can access thousands of movies and TV shows through the iPhone app (amazon.co.uk).

- **Netflix**: Watch movies and TV on your iPhone for a monthly fee (netflix.com).

- **YouTube**: There's a dedicated YouTube iPhone app available from the App Store, featuring billions of user-uploaded videos.

- **BBC iPlayer**: The iPlayer app allows users to get free access to recent (and selected older) BBC TV shows. Programming can be downloaded over Wi-Fi and watched offline.

- **Sky Go**: This allows live streaming of a host of channels (including Sky Sports, Sky Movies and Sky One) over Wi-Fi and 3G (you need to subscribe to Sky TV).

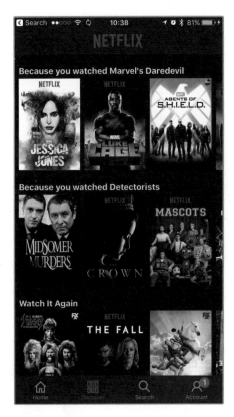

Above: The Netflix app allows you to stream thousands of movies and TV shows.

- **Now TV**: Want to just subscribe to a day, week or month of Sky content? Now TV is a great option.

READING

If you have an iPhone, you'll never be short of something to read – that's a promise. From brand-new bestsellers to classic books, the iBooks store is your oyster, while News offers access to the biggest stories of the day.

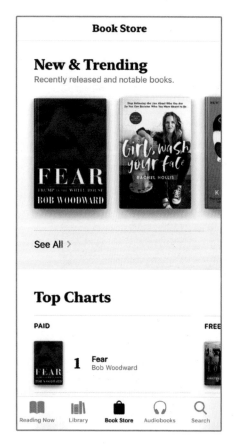

Above: The Books app.

BOOKS

Apple's digital bookstore, built into your iPhone, is called Book store (or iBooks in iOS 11 and earlier). It's all-new in iOS 12, so we'd encourage you up to update if you can. Here are the tabs you'll see when you open the app:

- **Reading Now**: Shows what you're currently reading, and offers a selection of featured content including books For You and What's Hot.

- **Library**: Shows a bookshelf of all your titles. Tapping a cover will open the book. Tapping Collections will allow you to sort between your wish list, finished books, audiobooks and more.

- **Store**: The Book Store tab features a host of featured and recommended titles, as well as the top charts and quick access to different genres.

- **Audiobooks**: Here you'll be able to discover new audiobooks and download them to listen at your leisure.

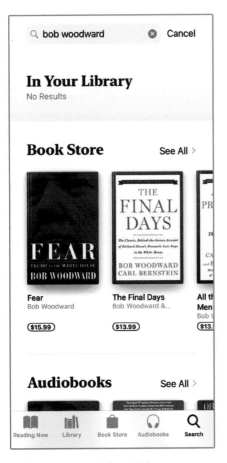

Above: You can search for a book by typing an author's name or book title into the search bar.

○ **Search**: Know what you're looking for? Head directly to the search tab and type in the name of a book or author to load the relevant titles.

Buying a Book

Once you've identified the book you want, you can buy it from the product page. Tap the Buy button, enter your Apple ID password and the book will appear on your bookshelf.

Book Samples

When browsing in a bookshop, it's natural to flick through a few pages before paying. The Book store has an equivalent through the Sample feature. On the product page, hit Sample and the book will open. Many will let you read the entire first chapter before committing to buying.

Right: When you select a book, you will be presented with the purchase option. Touch this button and authenticate the purchase to pay for the book and download it to your bookshelf.

**< Back**

Special Offers & Free

BESTSELLERS
Get your next book for less than the price of a latte.

$4

Our Picks: $3.99 or Less
Small investments with a big pay-off.

Reading Now | Library | **Book Store** | Audiobooks | Search

Above: There are many free books and special offers.

Hot Tip

In the Books app, you can see a 'want to read' button on each book's title page. This will add it to your wish list in Collections.

Free Books

Publishing laws mean that once a published book has been around for a certain amount of time, copyright expires and it becomes freely available. You can download free books from Charles Dickens, Jane Austen, William Shakespeare and more.

iCloud and Books

Apple's iCloud means that all previous purchases are available to read on your iPhone too. The Library tab lists the books that you have bought through iTunes on your computer or through the Books app on the iPad. Hit the Cloud icon to the right of the book to add these titles to your iPhone's bookshelf.

READING BOOKS

Now you have stocked your virtual bookshelf with a host of titles from the Books Store, it's time to start reading. Select the thumbnail cover from the Library to load the book full-screen on your device.

Turning Pages

The pages in Books turn as if you were reading a real book and it's one of the best-looking things you can do on an iPhone. Use your thumb to slowly drag from various points on the right side of the page to see this beautifully imagined feature in all its glory. You can also give the screen a little flick when you're ready to turn a page. Naturally, when going back a page, flick from left to right.

Finding a Page

If you're searching for a particular page within a book, there are a number of ways to reach it quickly:

- **Contents:** Tap the list icon at the top of the screen, where you can access the Contents page. Tap an item from the page to head to the beginning of that chapter.

- **Scan:** While reading tap the screen and you'll see a bar. Drag this to find specific pages. Take your finger off the screen when you've reached the page you want.

- **Search:** Hit the Search icon at the top of the screen and type in words or a page number. Make your selection from the list of results.

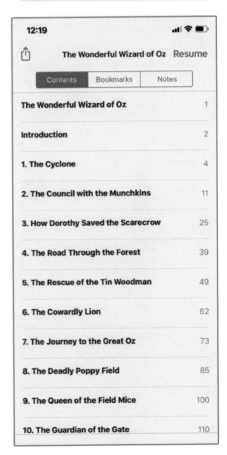

Above: Touch the List icon at the top of your screen to display the book's contents page.

- **Bookmarks:** You can add as many Bookmarks as you wish by pressing the icon at the top of the screen. All Bookmarks can be accessed by tapping the List icon and selecting the Bookmarks tab.

Changing the View

The Books app enables you to tailor your reading experience. Tap the middle of the screen to reveal the aA icon. Tap this to load the options, as follows:

Above: Touch the A icon to alter viewing options such as brightness and theme.

- **Brightness:** Rather than exiting the app to change the brightness, you can do it directly from the Books app.

- **Text size:** Hit the aA button to increase or decrease the size of the text.

- **Fonts:** Books boasts eight fonts. Pick your favourite from the list.

- **Themes:** Choose your desired colour scheme: black text on a white background, brown text on a sepia background or light grey text on a black background.

- **Auto Night:** Enabling this option will automatically convert the theme to white on black.

- **Scrolling View:** Turning on Scrolling View will allow you to read the book on a continuous page, rather than having to turn each page.

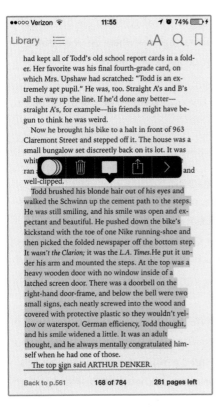

Above: You can select text sections to copy, define or highlight.

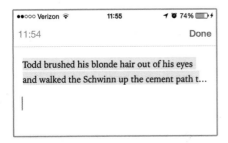

Above: You can paste highlighted sections into Notes.

Adding Highlights, Copying Text and Making Notes

Books also allows users to annotate the text with notes and highlights, while sections can also be copied and shared. In order to use these features, you'll need to select a piece of text. Hold the screen and move the two blue markers to highlight the relevant section of the text. You'll see an Options tab pop up, allowing you to do the following:

- **Copy**: This will copy a segment of the text, allowing you to paste it into another app (e.g. email, document, etc.).

- **Look Up**: If you've highlighted a particular word, you can ask Books for a dictionary definition.

- **Highlight**: Tapping Highlight will turn the section yellow, but it will also bring up a new Options screen, allowing you to change the colour, delete the highlight, share it or add a note.

- **Note**: This allows you to annotate text. The selected text will open in a new window. Type your notes and press Done to return to the page. To edit what you have written, tap the Post-it note next to the section.

- **Search:** Tapping Search will give you the option of searching for the passage elsewhere on your phone, or via the web (Google) or Wikipedia.

- **Share:** Share a favourite passage via the usual means.

KINDLE

Many people who graduate to using an iPhone own or have owned an Amazon Kindle ebook reader and are likely to have a library of digital books they've already bought. Thankfully, there's a Kindle app for the iPhone, where users can access all of their previous purchases.

The Kindle App

This application can be downloaded for free from the App Store (see page 160). Once you have opened it, enter your Amazon username and password, and select Register this Kindle. All of your previous purchases will be listed, so tap the cover to download each item. You can't buy books from the Kindle app; instead, you'll need to do that from amazon.com. Fret not though: after purchase, the books will still appear in the iPhone app.

Above: Enter your Amazon username and password and tap Register this Kindle to begin using the free app.

Reading a Kindle Book

Kindle Books can take advantage of Amazon's neat Whispersync technology, which means whenever you open a book in the Kindle app, it will sync to the last page you read on any of your devices. Beyond that, the means of reading books doesn't differ much from the Books app.

THE NEWS APP

With the News app, Apple wants to be the single repository for your daily news updates. Customise your feed and receive breaking news updates.

SETTING UP NEWS

When you tap News on the homescreen you'll need to go through a few set-up screens. The app will encourage you to choose your favourite topics and sources:

1. Choose whether you want to customise notifications.

2. Select whether you'd receive a daily email featuring a digest from Apple News editors.

3. Select whether you'd like Apple News to access your location. This will enable it to display local weather.

Making the Most of the News App

After selecting your preferences you'll see the News interface:

- **Today**: This shows a selection of top stories, trending news and customised stories depending on your preferences. Scroll down to see Editor's Picks, Top Videos and stories split into categories like Sport and Travel.

- **Spotlight**: A feature of stories that Apple thinks will be of interest to you, including Today's Top Read, Talking Points and In Pictures sections.

Above: You can Explore news sources and add them in order to see them in the Today section of the News app.

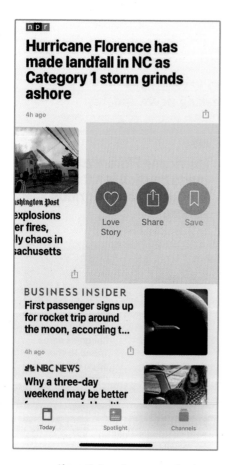

Above: Gestures allow you to work with stories without even opening them.

Channels: Here's where you can find new sources to add to your Today feed. There'll be recommendations and a chance to look at categories. Select the heart icon to add the channels.

Working with Articles in News

Tapping a news story will load the article page. You'll be able to scan it as you would a web page.

- Tap the aA icon at the top right to alter font size.

- Tap the Share icon at the foot of the screen to like, dislike, share and access regular sharing options.

- Tap the hearts to like/dislike a story. This will inform recommendations.

- Tap Next Story to move through the list.

Gestures in News

There's plenty you can do without even entering a news story, by swiping left and right on a story preview.

- **Swipe from right to left**: You'll see options to Love (Apple News will show more of this), Share or Save.

- **Swipe from left to right**: Tap to dislike (see less like this) or report inappropriate content.

- **Share**: You'll see a small share icon in the preview.

- **Next Story**: Once you've tapped an article preview to see the full story you can tap Next Story in the bottom right to move on.

News in the Today View

News is one of the helpful widgets within the Today screen (swipe right from the Home screen). You'll see Top, Trending and Videos stories tabs, enabling you to tap on individual stories.

Subscriptions

Some news sources keep their content behind a paywall, meaning you need to be a subscriber to access it. If you see this you can add your login details or hit Subscribe Now to do so from within the News app and pay via your Apple ID.

Managing Subscriptions

If you're paying to subscribe to News channels, Apple Music, Netflix or anything via your Apple ID account, you can manage these subscriptions within your Apple ID. Go to Settings > iTunes & App Store > Apple ID > View Apple ID. Authenticate your Apple ID and then tap Manage Subscriptions and select the one you wish to modify.

OTHER NEWS APPS

You can also obtain your news through stand-alone apps. The *Guardian*, the *Independent* and *Daily Star* all offer free apps. BBC News, Sky News and Channel 4 News also have apps that bring really great content from their broadcasts. All of these can be downloaded from the App Store.

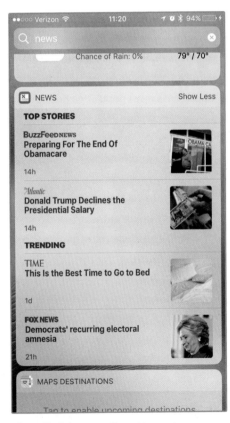

Above: The Today screen offers quick access to your feed via a News widget.

GAMING

All iPhone games are available to download from within the App Store and can be obtained using the methods explained in the previous chapter on apps.

PLAYING GAMES ON A TOUCH SCREEN

The multi-touch screen on the iPhone makes it a great gaming device. It means you can perform a host of swiping, tapping, zooming, pinching, dragging and flicking gestures using more than one digit at a time. The entire screen is your control pad and it helps to give each game its own uniqueness, while breathing new life into classic titles. We'll use a few of the App Store's most popular games as examples, to help you get started. See also the list of our favourites on page 252.

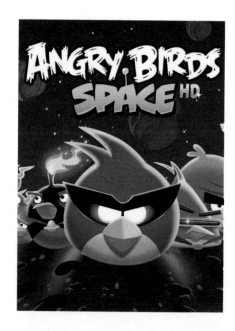

- **Line up and launch (e.g. Angry Birds):** Once you've downloaded the game from the App Store, it's easy to get started. Pull back the slingshot to aim the Angry Birds at the pigs and then release it to fire. You'll need to get the angle and the power right to hit your target.

- **Swipe and slash (e.g. Fruit Ninja):** Use your thumb or finger as a sword to slash the falling fruits in two. Once you get the hang of Fruit Ninja, try Infinity Blade, where you need to use a sword against a host of beasties from another world.

- **Drag and drop (e.g. Scrabble):** The classic Scrabble has been reinvented for the iPhone. You pick a letter

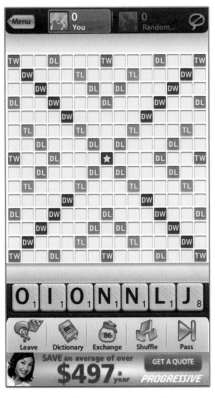

Above: Scrabble has been redesigned for the iPhone. Play by dragging and dropping letters.

and drag-and-drop it on to the board to form words, and the game will do the rest.

○ **Virtual buttons (e.g. FIFA 17)**: Scaled-down versions of Xbox One and PlayStation 4 games feature virtual buttons and directional arrows, which allow you to pass, shoot, tackle and move players.

○ **Tilting and turning (e.g. Asphalt 8)**: Racing games are amazing on the iPhone. With the gyroscopic sensor and built-in accelerometer, you can tilt the phone to steer the car left and right.

Above: Pokémon Go, a phenomenon in mobile gaming, uses the camera, GPS and the touchscreen.

Online Multiplayer Gaming

Many games allow for multiple participants. Some games, like Scrabble, have their own mechanisms for finding online opponents. More complex games are also emerging which allow you to play with others based on real world locations, for example Pokémon Go. Apple also has a back-end Game Center which helps to pair you up with partners over Wi-Fi.

CUSTOMIZING

The ability to personalize your handset, customizing how it looks and behaves, is one of the biggest draws of the iPhone. Like a made-to-measure suit, you can refine almost everything the iPhone does.

SETTINGS

To customize tools and apps, choose Settings from your Home screen. Here, you'll see a list of everything you can amend, from Wi-Fi and Sounds, to Privacy, Apps, Camera and more. Just click on the small > next to each item to dig deeper into its settings. You can access many of these settings just by swiping up from the foot of the screen to access the Control Center.

PREFERENCES

Airplane Mode

Using your mobile to make calls in-flight is frowned upon, but once you hit cruising altitude, you may want to listen to music, watch a film or play a game. In Settings, just toggle Airplane Mode on before you take off. This shuts down the phone's wireless functions, including Wi-Fi, 3G and 4G. A small Airplane icon will appear in the status bar to show you it's activated. You can also turn it on quickly in the Control Center – just swipe up from the Home screen to access it as normal.

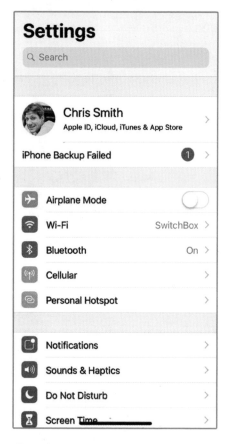

Above: The Settings page allows you to amend and customize many features.

Bluetooth Preferences

Bluetooth lets your iPhone communicate wirelessly with other devices such as headsets, fitness trackers, speakers or phones. You can switch it on and off in Control Center. However, in order to manage your Bluetooth setup, go to Settings and select Bluetooth. Managing which devices your iPhone can communicate with is simple:

- **To connect or disconnect a device**: Tap the name until the words Connected or Not Connected appear.

- **To unpair a device**: Tap the blue 'i', select Forget This Device and it will no longer appear in your list of available devices.

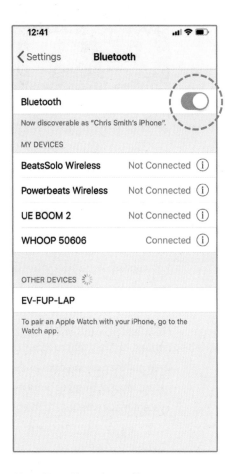

CONTINUITY

The idea is to improve the way iPhones work with Mac computers and iPad tablets. We'll discuss some examples of how Continuity can work. It's quite complex in terms of system requirements for each element, and if you're a PC user you won't be able to access any of them.

iPhone Cellular Calls

When you receive a phone call on your iPhone, you'll be able to answer it on a Mac or an iPad with Continuity.

> ## Hot Tip
> Ignored a Bluetooth device by mistake?
> Turn off your iPhone. When you reboot,
> the Bluetooth device you previously ignored
> will be back on the list.

Above: Turning Bluetooth on enables you to connect accessories like speakers and headphones.

Above: If you have a recent Mac as well as an iPhone, you'll be able to receive regular SMS messages on it.

You'll also be able to start calls from those devices if it's more convenient. This works with any iPhone/iPad on iOS 8 and up and any Mac with Mac OS X Yosemite and up.

SMS Relay

With Continuity enabled, when you get a text message from a non-iPhone device (e.g. an Android phone), that will also appear in your Messages app on Mac and iPad. This lets you to reply using the device closest to you. Conversations can be started using the means listed above for phone calls.

Instant Hotspot

If you're out of Wi-Fi range, you can share your iPhone's mobile data connection with your Mac or iPad using Continuity's Instant Hotspot feature. If you have the right gear running the right software, the iPhone's connection should automatically be available in the Wi-Fi menus on the iPad and Mac, allowing you to easily connect. If you don't have the tech necessary, you can still share your internet connection using Personal Hotspot (see page 228).

Handoff

With Handoff, you can start a task on one device and finish it on another. Within the context of Mail, that means you can start composing an email on one device and complete it on another when your handset is in Bluetooth range. It's not just Mail; it also works with Safari, Maps, Messages, Reminders, Calendar, Contacts, Pages, Numbers, and Keynote. System requirements are the same as Instant Hotspot listed above.

AirDrop

Another part of Continuity is AirDrop, a sharing technology that's available to some iPhone users. It can be used to exchange files with other iPhones, iPads (fourth generation or later) and newer Mac computers (running OS X Yosemite and up) in the near vicinity. You can enable AirDrop in the Command Center. Files can be shared from the Share icon in most apps, if compatible devices are within range of each other.

Above: If you're out of Wi-Fi range your iPad or Mac can connect to your iPhone's Personal Hotspot.

APPLE HOME

Imagine being able to dim the lights and lock the doors using only your phone? One of the new, advanced iPhone features is called Home. While still very much in the early days, there's a new HomeKit platform that's built into iOS. The idea is to use your iPhone to control a wealth of smart home devices, an emerging tech trend. You can already buy lights, locks, garage doors, thermostats, alarms and more. Everything is controlled via the Home app (from iOS 10).

Connecting a Home Device

We won't go into too much detail here. The set up process will differ slightly depending on which smart device you buy.

1. Plug in your new HomeKit enabled devices and follow the installation instructions to get it connected to the your home Wi-Fi network.

2. Make sure your iPhone is connected to the same Wi-Fi Network and open the Home app.

3. Tap the Add Accessory button in the app and it will search for compatible devices. Next you're likely to be asked to add a code that features on the device's packaging. Once complete you'll see the device within the Home app, listed as Online.

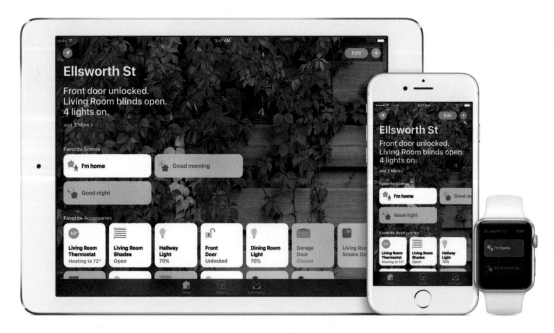

Above: You can control all manner of smart appliances in your home from an iPhone, iPad or Apple Watch.

The Home App

Once set-up, any HomeKit-enabled devices will live in the Home app. Here you'll also also be able to link devises with each other to create 'Scenes.' That could include a morning scene that adjusts a thermostat, brings up the lights and turns on the coffee pot with a single tap!

PRIVACY PREFERENCES

Your iPhone uses two methods to pinpoint where you are: built-in sat nav-style GPS or by triangulating signals from mobile phone masts and Wi-Fi points. These capabilities are used for everything, from helping you to navigate while using the Maps app to tagging photos you've taken with a location. If this is all a bit more Big Brother than you're happy with, you can go 'off the grid'. You can turn off Location Services completely by going to Settings > Privacy and toggling to Off.

Notifications Settings

iPhone Notifications provide a variety of different ways to alert you when something is received, updated or you've set a reminder. In addition to showing up as Alerts, Banners and Sounds, these updates also appear in the Notifications Center, which is accessed by swiping down from the top of the Home screen. You can fine-tune how and when your alerts appear in Notifications Settings.

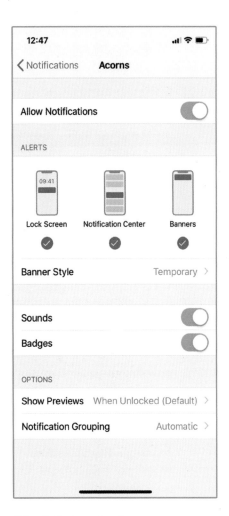

Above: Notification settings allow you to alter alerts for individual apps.

○ **To assign Notifications Settings for an app**: Go to Settings > Notifications and select the app from the list. You can then toggle the Sounds, Alerts, Banners and Badges

to On or Off for that app, and
decide whether the alerts appear in
the main Notification Center.

Sound Settings

Go to Settings > Sounds. Here, you can switch
audio alerts on or off, for everything from
incoming email through to calendar alerts.
You can also assign each function its own tone,
manage your ringtones, set volume levels and
decide whether or not your phone should
vibrate when you have an alert.

SIRI

In Settings > Siri you can choose the language
Siri speaks, decide whether you want voice
feedback, and teach it more about you by
providing personal information under My Info.
This will let you to say, for example, 'Siri, take
me home' to load directions in Maps. You can
also choose whether you want to enable the
hands-free 'Hey Siri' feature.

'Hey Siri'

A feature in iOS 8 and up is the ability to
access Siri without holding down the Home
button. If you enable this in Settings, you'll
be able to say 'Hey Siri' to summon the app
whenever you want.

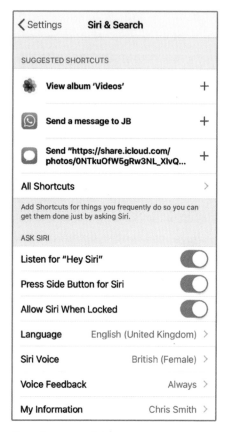

Above: Siri settings include language
and voice-feedback options.

**If you can't find something
you're looking for in Settings,
scroll to the top and type it in
the search bar.**

GENERAL SETTINGS

Many of the features in this book can be altered in the Settings > General section. Here, you'll find information about software updates, Siri, Usage, iTunes Wi-Fi Sync and more.

About

Want to know how many songs, photos and apps are on your phone? Or how much space you have left? You need to check out the About section in Settings > General, which is where all the nitty-gritty but important details about your phone live. Other things you'll find here include: software version (e.g. iOS 12), model and serial numbers, Wi-Fi address and network information.

Software Update

Head here to find out if there's a software update to download and install for your phone. See page 44 for information on how to update your phone.

iTunes Wi-Fi Sync

You can sync your iPhone to a PC or Mac without needing to physically connect the device with a USB cable. If Wi-Fi syncing has been set up in iTunes (see page 41 for syncing via iTunes), a Sync Now button will appear. Hit this and your devices will do their thing.

Keyboard

You can change the way your iPhone keyboard works; go into Settings > General > Keyboard. There, you can enable many special functions, such as Auto-Capitalization, Enable Caps Lock and Auto Correction. You can also add an international keyboard.

Below: Keyboard settings can be used to turn on predictive text and spell checking, among other settings.

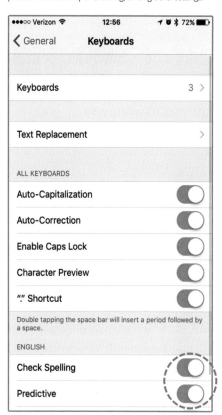

New Keyboards

Not happy with the standard iPhone keyboard? You can install your own from the App Store. This means you can use keyboards like Gboard that harnesses the power of Google search. Once you've downloaded it, you will need to go to Settings > General > Keyboard > Add New Keyboard and select the new keyboard from the list to install it. When typing a message or email, select the Globe icon to switch between the keyboards.

Above: Gboard is an alternative keyboard which harnesses the power of Google Search.

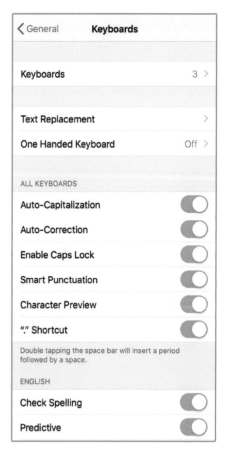

Above: Keyboard settings can be used to turn on predictive text and spell checking, among other settings.

Reset Settings

Only the brave, the desperate or the foolish mess around with the Reset settings (Settings > General > Reset). Luckily, you'll need a password before you can hit the big red buttons, but here's what each of them does, should you decide to proceed:

- **Reset All Settings**: Resets your settings to default, but does not affect your data or media.

- **Erase All Content and Settings**: Deletes all data and resets the settings to default.

- **Reset Network Settings**: Restores your phone's network settings to the factory defaults.

- **Reset Keyboard Dictionary**: Removes any words you may have added to the dictionary accidentally.

- **Reset Home Screen Layout**: Makes your Home screen factory fresh, with apps re-arranged to the factory settings.

- **Reset Location & Privacy**: Restores default settings for location and privacy.

Above: Remember to switch off Data Roaming when travelling abroad to save on costly charges.

Data Roaming

Some UK networks now let you use your phone contract abroad as you would at home without incurring charges. If you're not among these customers then leaving your

Create your own keyboard short cuts to make typing faster. Go into Settings > Keyboard and Add Shortcuts. You'll be able to type things like 'GTBL' and the full text 'Going to be late' will appear as a suggestion as you type.

●●○○○ Verizon LTE ◌   12:54   ✈ ⚡ ✱ 73% ▬

❮ Cellular   **Personal Hotspot**

Personal Hotspot   ⬤▭

Now Discoverable.
Other users can look for your shared network using Wi-Fi and Bluetooth under the name "iPhone 6".

Wi-Fi Password   pontesbury ❯

📶   TO CONNECT USING WI-FI
     1 Choose "iPhone 6" from the Wi-Fi settings on your
       computer or other device.
     2 Enter the password when prompted.

✱   TO CONNECT USING BLUETOOTH
     1 Pair iPhone with your computer.
     2 On iPhone, tap Pair or enter the code displayed on
       your computer.
     3 Connect to iPhone from computer.

🔌   TO CONNECT USING USB
     1 Plug iPhone into your computer.
     2 Choose iPhone from the list of network services in
       your settings.

Above: If your network provider allows it, you can enable Personal Hotspot to share your data connection with other devices.

Hot Tip
A shortcut to the Personal Hotspot settings exists within the Control Center.

data switched on can be a costly business. Go into Settings > Cellular > Cellular Data Options > Roaming and toggle data roaming switch to off.

Personal Hotspot
If you're in a no-Wi-Fi zone, you can share the iPhone's internet connection with a computer, iPhone or iPad, provided your network allows it (or you pay extra for the privilege!). To enable this, go into Settings > Cellular and select Personal Hotspot and toggle the button on or off as required. This will see the iPhone show up as a Wi-Fi network for other devices. To connect, you can give them the password generated within Personal Hotspot.

TROUBLESHOOTING

Even good gadgets go wrong, and the iPhone isn't immune to the odd glitch. This section will help you to overcome most of the problems you're likely to encounter.

CONNECTIVITY

Bugs are often fixed by iOS updates, but if you can't wait for new software, there are techy solutions on the web – be warned though: these tend to be complicated. So before you start meddling with DNS settings, here are some simple cures to most connection quibbles.

Wireless

Here are some checks to run through if you're having problems connecting to the Wi-Fi:

- **Is Wi-Fi enabled?** Tap Settings > Wi-Fi and make sure that Wi-Fi is turned on.

- **Connected to a network?** No? Pick an available Wi-Fi network from the list you'll find under Choose a Network and tap the one you want to join.

- **Entered a password?** Double-check that your password is correct.

- **Check the signal**: The Wi-Fi icon in the status bar shows a varying number of bars to indicate the signal strength. More bars equal a stronger signal.

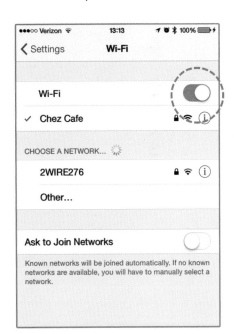

Above: If you are having connectivity problems, check your Wi-Fi settings.

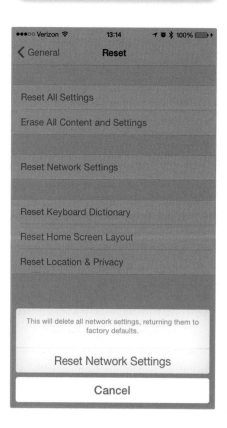

iPhone Reset screen:

●●●○○ Verizon 📶   13:14   ➤ 🔵 ⚡ 100% 🔋⚡

< General   **Reset**

Reset All Settings

Erase All Content and Settings

Reset Network Settings

Reset Keyboard Dictionary

Reset Home Screen Layout

Reset Location & Privacy

This will delete all network settings, returning them to factory defaults.

Reset Network Settings

Cancel

○ **Weak signal?** Move closer to your router or Wi-Fi point and remember that brick walls, and other interferences can affect the signal.

○ **Can you browse the web?** Launch a browser to test the web connection. Navigate to an easy-to-load page like google.co.uk.

○ **Check your Wi-Fi network:** If the status bar shows you're connected but web content won't load, it suggests a problem with the Wi-Fi network you're using. If you're at home, check the cable connection to your Wi-Fi router or try connecting another device to the network to test it.

○ **Reset network settings:** This will clear your 3G and Wi-Fi network settings, including saved networks, Wi-Fi passwords and VPN settings, so it is a last resort. Tap Settings > General and then scroll down and press Reset > Reset Network Settings. When the phone reboots, find and join the Wi-Fi network again.

Phone

If you're having trouble making or receiving calls and texts, try the following:

Left: Resetting network settings should be a last resort when solving connectivity problems.

- **Airplane Mode**: Swipe up on the Home screen to bring up the Control Center and make sure the airplane icon is not lit.

- **Signal**: In the top left-hand corner you'll see the signal bar. The more bars, the stronger the signal. If you're only seeing one or two bars, calls and texts might not work.

- **Location**: If you're inside, head outside. Or, if you're already outside, chase that phone signal!

- **Switch Airplane Mode on and off**: Go to Settings and toggle Airplane Mode on and then off. This resets your wireless data connections and can flush out any related problems.

- **Restart your phone**: Yes, we know it's an old trick, but it often works.

- **SIM card**: With your phone switched off, remove the SIM tray and take out the SIM card and reposition. Reinsert the tray and restart the phone.

- **Restore your phone**: Still no joy? The next step is to restore your phone (*see* page 242 to find out how this is done).

Above: If the Wi-Fi symbol is lit in blue in the Control Center then it is enabled.

Hot Tip
The problem might be with your network provider – if you can access the web it's worth checking their website.

SYNCING

This section looks at problems that can occur while syncing your iPhone with iTunes and iCloud and any gremlins preventing your computer from recognizing the existence of your handset.

iTunes

When connecting your device to your computer an iPhone icon should appear in iTunes in the top menu. If this doesn't happen, then here is what you can do:

- ○ **Update iTunes**
- ○ **Restart your phone**
- ○ **Recharge your phone**
- ○ **Restart your computer**
- ○ **Uninstall and reinstall iTunes**

iTunes Syncing Over Wi-Fi

You can sync your iPhone with iTunes over the air and go fully cable-free. For this to work you'll need

Above: On phones with a Home button restart the phone by pressing and holding the power and Home buttons, until the Apple logo appears and then release.

Hot Tip

Using iCloud rather than iTunes to sync and back up photos means that your pictures will be automatically updated when you join a Wi-Fi network (*see* page 42 for more iCloud benefits).

your computer running iTunes and your iPhone to be connected to a power source and the same Wi-Fi network. If that's all present and correct and you're still having problems, there are some crucial checks you need to make:

- **Ensure Wi-Fi sync is enabled in Settings > General > Wi-Fi Sync**
- **Quit iTunes and restart**
- **Restart your network router**
- **Check your network connection**
- **Check your firewall settings**

Not Enough Free Space

Whether you're syncing over Wi-Fi or via USB/Lightning, you might encounter the following message: 'iPhone cannot be synced because there is not enough free space to hold all of the items in the iTunes Library (additional space required)'. To fix this, try turning off the automatic syncing function in iTunes, as shown here:

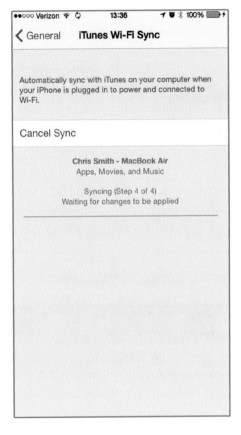

Above: You can sync content from your iTunes Library to your iPhone over Wi-Fi.

- **Select your iPhone**: In the iTunes navigation bar, find your iPhone and click the Summary tab.

- **Turn off Auto Sync**: Deselect Automatically sync when this iPhone is connected and select the Sync only ticked songs and videos tickbox. Click Apply: this will sync the changes to your iPhone.

Above: If you run out of free space, you should deselect the option to Automatically sync when this iPhone is connected. Instead, you should select the option to Sync only ticked songs and videos.

○ **Sync less data**: If syncing your entire music library exceeds the memory capacity of your iPhone, then choose Selected playlists to transfer rather than All songs and playlists under the Music tab in iTunes. You can also manage apps, films and Books in the same way.

Hot Tip

Having trouble syncing over Wi-Fi? Check that your iPhone is connected to the same Wi-Fi network as your Mac or PC, as it won't work if it isn't. Your iPhone will also need to be plugged into a power source.

iCLOUD

iCloud is great for backing up all of your favourite content and being able to access it from any Apple device (and some non-Apple devices), but it's also a complicated beast if it goes wrong. As there are far too many troubleshooting issues to cover here in detail, we'll show you how to spot and fix the most common troubles (also try apple.com/support/icloud).

Hot Tip

Ensure you have at least 50 MB free space available on your iPhone before you attempt to back up. If you have no space available, iCloud Backup can fail.

- **Can't sign into iCloud?** Make sure you're using the Apple ID email address you used when you set up your iCloud account. If you've forgotten your password, you can reset it online at appleid.apple.com.

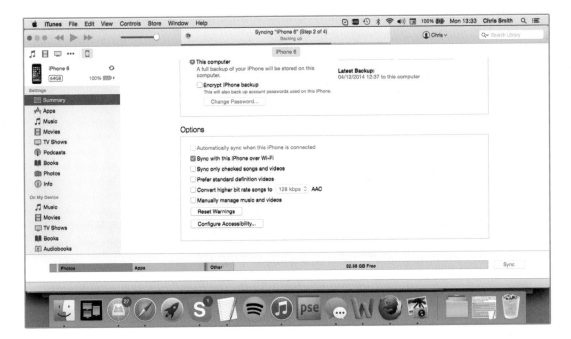

Above: You can check and adjust your backup settings through the Summary section of your iTunes account.

- **Automatic backups won't start?** These only start when your iPhone is plugged into a power source, connected to Wi-Fi and the screen is locked. You can start a backup manually by tapping Back Up Now in Settings > Your Name > iCloud > Storage & Backup.

- **Out of cloud storage space?** If you're told you don't have enough cloud storage space, try excluding your Camera Roll and other large data items from backups. If that's not fixing the problem, you can always buy more storage to add to the free 5 GB provided by Apple.

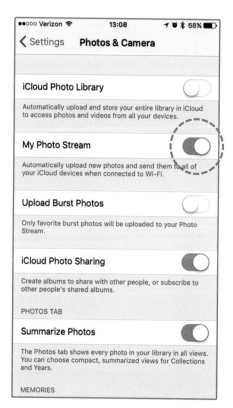

Above: You can check and adjust your Photo Stream settings.

- **My photos are not appearing in My Photo Stream:** From your iPhone's Home screen, select Settings > Your Name > iCloud > Photos > My Photo Stream and make sure that the slider is on, then make sure that you're connected to a Wi-Fi network. Photo Stream won't upload photos from an iOS device until the Camera app is closed on the device you used to take the photo, so check this. Also ensure your iPhone battery hasn't dropped below 20 per cent, as Photo Stream downloading and uploading are disabled when the battery reaches this threshold.

iCLOUD DRIVE

One of the reasons you may need more storage space is if you're using iCloud Drive. If you remeber during set-up Apple asked if we'd like to use it. It is an online-based storage locker, which allows you to access any of your files on multiple Apple devices and at iCloud.com. If you don't have a Mac computer, it's not that much use, so you can probably skip this section.

Setting up iCloud Drive

Firstly, you'll need an iPhone running iOS 8 and up and a Mac computer running OS X Yosemite and up. If you do, head to Settings > iCloud and turn on iCloud Drive. On your Mac go to System Preferences > iCloud and tick the iCloud Drive. An iCloud Drive tab will appear in your Finder Window.

Sharing Files to iCloud Drive

If you've ever used Dropbox, iCloud Drive works in the same way. The idea is that items saved to iCloud Drive will be synced across multiple devices, allowing you to work with one version that's accessible wherever you are. You can share any file as long as it's less than 15 GB in size, and it can be picked up on your iPhone in compatible programs like Pages, Numbers and Keynote.

Finding iCloud Drive Files

iCloud Drive files live within the Files app in iOS 11 and up. Here you'll find content from apps like Pages, Numbers, Keynote as well as any images or PDFs you have saved. You can view and edit and any changes will be automatically synced back to your Mac.

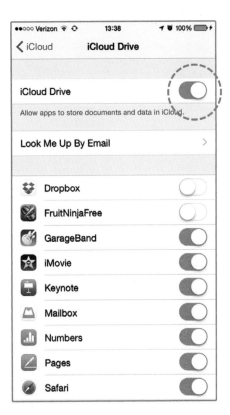

Above: iCloud Drive allows you to access files on all of your Apple devices.

APPS

Most of the apps in the App Store work well – most of the time. However, even the best-maintained apps can be prone to bugs; from crashing to sluggish performance, here's what to do when your apps aren't working:

Above: Multitasking screen showing which apps are live.

○ **Close the app:** If an app gets stuck during loading, you can bump-start it. Access the multitasking menu to see a list of all open apps. Scroll to find the rogue app, then just swipe its card up off the screen and reopen the app as normal.

○ **Update the app:** Sometimes apps become glitchy because the developers have released an update. Go to App Store > Updates to check.

○ **Reset your iPhone:** Resetting fixes 95 per cent of glitches. Reset your phone by holding the Power and volume down (or Home, if you have one) buttons simultaneously for 10 seconds and open the app again.

○ **Delete and reinstall the app:** Press down on the app icon until an x appears over it; press it and confirm you want to delete the app. Once it's gone, you can then reinstall it.

BATTERY

If your iPhone battery is winding up empty too quickly, you might have a faulty battery. However, it's more likely that your settings and usage are drinking more power than necessary. Here are some simple ways to make your iPhone last longer:

○ **Drain the battery:** About once a month, let the phone run until it shuts down on its own and then charge it back up to full.

○ **Close background apps:** Access your phone's multitasking menu to see a series of cards representing open apps. Swipe each card up and off the screen to close it.

- **Push Notifications**: If lots of Push notifications are enabled, they can wear down your battery by constantly checking for updates. Go to Settings > Notifications and click on the apps from which you don't need notifications. The Mail app is a particular culprit.

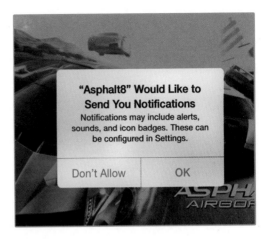

"Asphalt8" Would Like to Send You Notifications
Notifications may include alerts, sounds, and icon badges. These can be configured in Settings.

Don't Allow   OK

- **A weak mobile data signal**: Your phone works harder when it's struggling to find a 3G/4G signal. If you're going to be in an area with bad coverage for a long period, switch on Airplane Mode.

Above: Apps will often request permission to send you push notifications.

- **Turn off 4G LTE**: Using 4G internet is a bigger drain on the battery. Head to Settings > Cellular and toggle off the Enable LTE setting.

- **Location Services**: If you don't need your location pinpointed, go to Settings > Location Services and choose which apps you want to use location.

- **Turn off Background App Refresh**: You can toggle individual apps through Settings > General > Background App Refresh.

- **Turn Wi-Fi/Bluetooth off**: The constant search for Wi-Fi networks drains power. Newer iPhones use Bluetooth 4.0 which consumes less power, but it still has an impact.

- **Update your iOS software**: Each version of iOS tends to deliver battery life improvements, so make sure you're running the latest version.

- **Dynamic wallpaper**: Switch this to something solid in the wallpapers section.

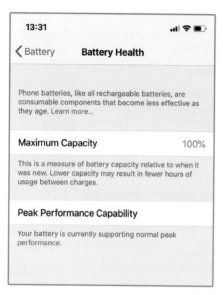

Above: The iPhone now features a Battery Health section.

Battery Health

Your battery has a finite number of charges. In iOS 11.3 Apple added a new Battery Health feature (Settings > Battery > Battery Health) which gives your battery a Maximum Capacity score. If your battery has degraded and needs replacing, this screen will let you know.

Low Power Mode

Apple has added a new tool called Low Power Mode. When enabled it will turn off Email fetch, Hey Siri, Background app refresh, Automatic downloads and some visual effects to save your battery. You can manually enable it from Settings > Battery if your battery is under 80% charged. When your battery reaches 20% capacity you'll also receive an alert asking whether you want to turn it on.

FROZEN iPHONE

If your phone completely locks up, follow these simple steps to get it back up and running:

- ○ **Recharge:** Make sure your phone is fully charged. Turn it off while it's charging and use the mains charger. If a full battery doesn't cure the seizure, it's time to reboot.

- ○ **Force reboot:** Press and hold the Power button while simultaneously pressing and holding the Home button (on iPhone 7 and below). On an iPhone 8, X and up quickly press volume up, then volume down and hold the power button. You should see the Apple logo appear. After that, let go and your phone will reset.

- ○ **Restore:** Restoring your phone is not something you do lightly, but if you've tried the options above and all that has failed, then it might be your only option. Before you start, back up your phone if you can. Next follow these steps:

1. Connect your phone to your computer like you would if you were syncing. When iTunes opens, select the Summary tab and click the Restore button.

2. Re-sync your phone to restore your data. You'll have to go through setup again and select from Restore from iTunes Backup or Restore from iCloud backup, depending on which you use.

○ **Recovery**: If recharging, restarting, resetting and restoring haven't fixed your fault, the final option is to put your phone into Recovery Mode:

1. Make sure you're using the latest version of iTunes on your computer. If iTunes is open, close it. Next connect your iPhone to your computer and open iTunes.

2. Force restart your iPhone as explained on the previous page, but keep the buttons pressed down when the Apple logo appears. You should see a Connect to iTunes screen.

3. Release any buttons when the Connect to iTunes screen appears. iTunes should launch automatically, but if it hasn't, open it manually.

4. You should see the option to Restore or Update options. Try to update first as this will protect your data. If this fails, hit Restore. You'll have to set up your device again afterwards.

RUNNING OUT OF SPACE

Once you start downloading apps, games, music, films and photos, it's easy to fill up your iPhone's storage. There are many ways to manage your content more smartly to free up space.

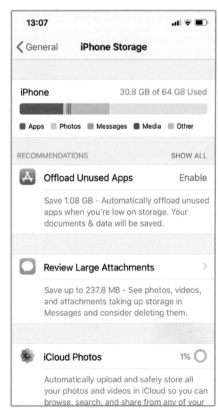

Above: Checking the iPhone storage screen in General Settings can inform you what's taking up all your space.

Managing Storage Space

Find out what's using your storage: Head to Settings > General > iPhone Storage. Tap Manage Storage to see what's filling up the space:

- **Offload unused apps**: Ditch those space hogs. This will delete the app itself but retain the data associated with it. The app will appear greyed out on the homescreen in this instance, so just tap to redownload.

- **Review Large Attachments**: Photos, videos and other attachments sent by others take up space on your phone too. Here you can review all files individually and delete them.

- **App List**: You can manage the storage used by individual apps on the iPhone Storage settings screen. For example, the Podcast app might be hogging space with episodes you've already heard. You can delete them here.

- **Remove old videos**: Storing an iTunes Movie? Get rid of it, you can always re-download it.

Switch to Streaming

A great way to free up space on your iPhone is to switch to web-based options for music and video. You don't need to store all that iTunes music on your phone if you can stream it over Wi-Fi using Apple Music or Spotify.

Above: You can close down apps by swiping them off screen in the multitasking view in order to speed up the performance of your iPhone.

SECURITY

The iPhone is an expensive piece of technology. Keeping the physical product safe is essential, but it's just as important to protect the data and information stored on your phone.

PROTECTION

We've set up Passcodes and a Touch ID fingerprint to protect the phone, while our Apple IDs also have their own passwords. This should keep your iPhone safe should it call into the wrong hands. However, here are some additional steps.

Failed Passcode Data Dump

From the same Settings > Touch ID/Face ID and Passcode menu, you can set the iPhone to automatically Erase Data if someone makes 10 failed attempts at unlocking your phone with the passcode. Be warned: all your media, data, settings and information will be deleted, so think carefully before you activate this.

Touch ID and Face ID

Within the same menu, you can add an additional digital for unlocking your phone with a fingerprint, which makes it easier to unlock with both hands and if you share the device with another family member. For Face ID you can add an Alternate Appearance. In this screen you can also decide whether you want

Above: You can choose your own passcode to increase security.

Touch ID/Face ID to use Touch ID to authorise iTunes and App Store purchases, Apple Pay, Password Autofill options in Safari and other compatible applications like banking and shopping apps.

Face ID and Touch ID with Other Apps

Rather than inserting your password every time you want to log onto your banking account, some apps will let you use Touch ID/Face ID to prove your identity. Once you've logged on for the first time you may be asked if you want to enable Face ID/Touch ID. Those apps with permissions will appear within the Touch ID/Face ID & Passcode settings. Here you can chose to turn off those permissions.

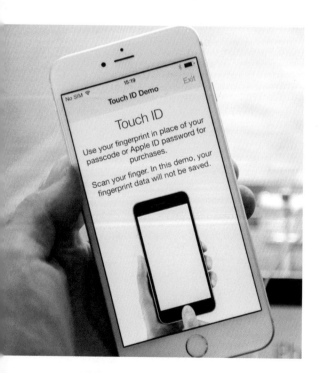

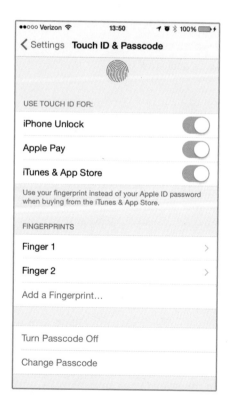

Above: Setting up an additional Touch ID fingerprint can be useful if more than one member of your household uses the device.

30 Seconds	
1 Minute	✓
2 Minutes	
3 Minutes	
4 Minutes	
5 Minutes	
Never	

Above: Protect your phone's battery life and your data by ensuring the display quickly locks down when not in use.

Hot Tip

The Settings app can feel complex, with lots of menus. If you can't find what you're looking for try searching for the setting at the very top of the main page.

Auto-Lock

To make your phone lock itself if it has been sitting idle, go into Settings > Display & Brightness > Auto-Lock and you can set the amount of time that elapses since your phone was last used before it automatically locks the display. Your options range from five minutes down to one minute. Selecting Never will quickly drain your battery.

SIM Locking

Any data that might be stored on your SIM card – anything from phone numbers to photos – can also be protected with a PIN code. Go to Settings > Phone and turn on SIM PIN and enter a password; this will prevent anyone else from using it in another phone without knowing the magic code.

Restrictions

The iPhone's restrictions tools let you dictate what can and can't be done with your phone. This is handy if the device is being used by a child. From locking the Safari web browser to preventing new apps being loaded on to the device, it's possible to manage the phone in a way that adds layers of safety, security and parental guidance. Head to Settings > Screen Time > Content & Privacy Restrictions to create a Restrictions Passcode, then you can turn off access to certain apps and certain iTunes content (such as music with explicit lyrics).

ENCRYPTING BACKUP

Whenever you connect your iPhone to iTunes to sync, update or restore your device, most of your essential data is backed up to your computer's hard drive or to iCloud. This includes photos, text messages, notes, contact favourites and some settings. It's possible to keep this data safe from unwanted prying eyes by encrypting your backups for an added level of security.

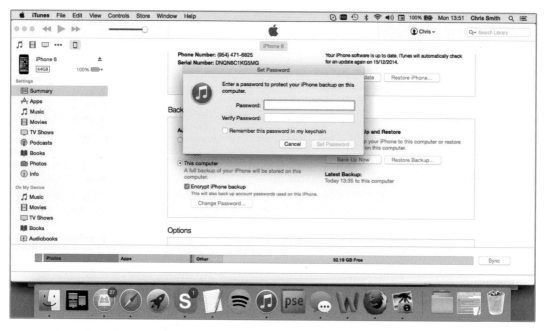

Above: You can choose to encrypt your iPhone data by selecting the Encrypt iPhone backup option from the menu in the iTunes summary tab.

Encrypt Your Data

If you choose to back up your iPhone to your computer, you get the option to encrypt and password-protect your data. It's simple to do. Just connect your handset to your computer and open iTunes. Load the iPhone and in the summary section, click Back up to This computer and tick the box that says Encrypt iPhone backup.

Find My iPhone

Your phone is now secured. If it's lost and stolen, it's unlikely that anyone will be able to access your important data. If you want to get it back or erase the data permanently then Find My iPhone is your friend. Go to iCloud > Find My iPhone and turn it On.

1. From any device you'll be able to go to iCloud.com and login using your Apple ID.

2. Select Find My iPhone. If the device is switched on you'll be able to choose Devices and select the iPhone to see its location on the map. If you think it may be in the vicinity press Play Sound to help you locate it.

3. Selecting Lost Mode will lock the device while still allowing you to track the device. It'll also allow you to compose a message to place on the Lockscreen containing contact information should it be found.

4. If you've lost hope you can completely erase all data on the iPhone by selecting Erase iPhone.

Above: Find My iPhone will help you locate an errant device and, if the worst comes to the worst, erase your data.

Physically Protecting Your Device

Now the software is protected, you'll also want to physically protect your iPhone. There are two major ways to do so, with a case and a screen saver. Do not scrimp on these. It's worthwhile to get high quality products in the long run. Even if you have AppleCare or insurance, there'll likely be a fee or deductible involved with repair.

Go to Settings > Your Name > iCloud > Find My iPhone to ensure your phone records its last known location before the battery dies.

TOP 100 APPS

This is our list of the top 100 apps we think that every iPhone user should have, or aspire to have. Some are essentials; others are those that you might use only occasionally but are what brings your iPhone to life. Have a look through our picks and see what your iPhone is missing out on.

Shopping

1.   **eBay**: Sell or buy and find out instantly when a bid has been successful. **Free.**

2.   **Amazon Mobile**: Use the iPhone camera to take a picture of a product to see if it's in stock. **Free.**

3.   **Etsy**: Shop online for home crafted arts and goods. **Free.**

4.   **Expedia**: Book your flights, hotels and rental cars in one fell swoop. **Free.**

5.   **Groupon**: Get special offers on experiences and events, depending on your current location. **Free.**

6.   **Starbucks**: Pay for your coffee wirelessly with your digital Starbucks card and save towards rewards. **Free.**

7.   **PayPal**: Send money, make payments, check your account details and more. **Free.**

Connectivity

8.   **WhatsApp**: The multi-platform messaging app which allows you to freely chat with friends with any phone, over the internet.

9.   **Chrome**: Supports unlimited tabs and can send pages from your computer to your iPhone. **Free.**

10.   **Outlook**: Microsoft's email client is useful and one of the best alternatives to the stock Mail app.

11.   **Skype**: Make free voice calls, video conversations and instant messaging. **Free.**

12.   **Gmail**: Native email client for Gmail users that's easy to use and set up. **Free.**

Watch and Listen

13.   **Podcasts**: Download, subscribe and listen to your favourite podcasts.

14.   **Now TV**: Buy daily, weekly or monthly access to premium Sky content. **Free.**

15.   **BBC iPlayer**: Catch up on BBC TV programmes and radio. **Free.**

16.   **4oD**: Channel 4's TV on-demand service lets you catch up with their shows. **Free.**

17.   **Songkick Concerts**: Be alterted when your favourite bands are in town. **Free.**

18.   **Virgin TV Anywhere**: Virgin TiVo customers can watch live TV over a Wi-Fi connection. **Free.**

19.   **Movies by Flixster**: Get your local movie showtimes, buy tickets, check reviews, watch trailers and more. **Free.**

20.   **Netflix**: Pay a monthly subscription and watch TV shows and films in full HD.

21.   **Amazon Prime Instant Video**: Amazon Prime members can choose from over 70,000 TV shows and movies from the US and the UK.

Free

22.   **Apple Remote**: Take control of iTunes or Apple TV and select playlists or adjust volume. **Free.**

23.   **YouTube**: Browse and watch millions of videos from the most popular video sharing site in the world. **Free.**

24. **iHeartRadio**: Access to a huge network of radio stations online. **Free.**

25. **Spotify**: Premium subscribers stream music over mobile data and Wi-Fi, and save playlists offline without being connected to the internet. **Free.**

26. **TuneIn Radio**: With access to over 60,000 global radio stations, you can pause live streams to re-listen to favourite shows. **Free.**

27. **iPlayer Radio**: The iPlayer for audio, it has access to 300 UK radio stations including your favourite BBC stations. **Free.**

28. **Shazam**: Hold the Shazam app up to a song and it will tell you all you need to know about the track. **Free.**

Reading

29. **The Guardian**: Offering access to the latest content from the British newspaper. **Free.**

30. **NPR**: Independent news and audio content from the United States. **Free**

31. **Feedly**: This attractive RSS reader aggregates all of your favourite stories from around the web in one place. **Free.**

32. **BBC News**: Access content from one of the world's most reputable news services. **Free.**

33. **Flipboard**: Keep up with news stories you are interested in with your personlised news app. **Free.**

34. **Pocket**: Pocket syncs to your device so you can catch up on articles when it is convenient. **Free.**

35. **iBooks**: Apple's official ebook store lets you buy and read a variety of books. **Free.**

36. **Kindle**: Read Kindle books, newspapers and magazines on your iPhone. **Free.**

Social Media

37. **Snapchat**: Messaging app that allows you to quickly share photos and videos that disappear within a set timeframe. Popular among younger iPhone users. **Free.**

38. **Facebook**: The friend-collecting site will let you update your status, check your news feed and receive notifications of posts. **Free.**

39. **Twitter**: Tweet on the go with the new Discover feature helping find suitable tweets and people to follow. **Free.**

40. **LinkedIn**: Giving you access to your entire professional network. **Free.**

41. **Periscope**: Live stream video to the world and then replay them whenever you like. Get responses from your viewers as you broadcast. **Free.**

42. **Tweetbot**: An alternative way to enjoy Twitter, if you get bored with the official app.

43. **Tumblr**: A great app for following your favourite blogs, sharing content and posting to your own. **Free.**

44. **Tinder**: A dating app that allows you to select potential suitors by swiping left and right on their pictures. **Free.**

Photos and Video

45. **Hipstamatic**: Produce retro-looking Polaroid-style photos with your iPhone. **£0.69.**

46. **Instagram**: Add filters to photographs to give them a vintage look, and share with other users via Facebook or Twitter. **Free.**

47. **Google Photos**: Back up all of your photos with unlimited storage and inventive album creation. **Free.**

48. **Adobe Photoshop Touch**: Includes many of the creative tools in the desktop version to modify and enhance images. **Free.**

49. **Dropbox**: Access files wherever you are, as well as offline, upload video and photos in bulk. **Free.**

50. **Pinterest**: Create boards and 'pin' images from the web to show the world what inspires you. **Free.**

51. **Flickr:** The photo-sharing app that now supports video will let you upload multiple content. **Free.**

52: **iMovie:** Edit and stitch together video clips, add captions and a soundtrack and upload the finished article to YouTube. **Free.**

53. **Moonpig:** Upload photos from your iPhone to create a unique card that can then be sent to the desired address. **Free.**

Geo-Location and Travel

54. **Google Maps:** If you're not happy with Apple Maps, you can download Google Maps and access great features like Street View. **Free.**

55. **Find My Friends:** Locate contacts with an iPhone, iPad or other Apple device to make meeting up easier. **Free.**

56. **Google Earth:** Search places from around the world with detailed maps. **Free.**

57. **Uber:** Book a ride through your iPhone and be notified when it arrives (certain UK locations only). **Free.**

58. **Dark Sky:** The most attractive, awesome weather app you're ever likely to see. It'll let you know the conditions up to an hour in advance. **£2.49.**

59. **Trip Advisor:** Offers a complete offline guide to cities, with visitor attraction details. **Free.**

60. **Flight Track:** You can check the status of your flight: real-time departures, gate closing times and alternative flights. **£2.99.**

61. **Airbnb:** Tired of staying in samey hotels? Find an actual house for your week in the countryside. **Free.**

62. **Open Table:** Reserve a seat at restaurants around town and discover local gems wherever you are. **Free.**

63. **The Trainline:** Check live train times, view your next train home and buy tickets. **Free.**

64. **Google Translate:** Brilliant translation app that'll convert language on the fly and even read signs. **Free.**

Sport and Fitness

65. **Apple Health:** The built-in Health app will count your steps and bring in data from various fitness tracking devices once they are set up. **Free.**

66. **Endomondo:** One of the best apps, for keeping tabs on your workout information. **Free.**

67: **Runkeeper:** Track your running and cycling activity, see your route on a map and get information on distance and calories burned. **Free.**

68. **Couch to 5K:** A great app to gently get you started with running if you haven't done so in a while! **Free.**

69: **Fitbit:** Connect your fitness tracker to the official app to see all of your fitness data. **Free.**

70. **Headspace:** Guided meditation sessions to get you started, with 10 free sessions.

71. **Calorie Counter & Diet Tracker:** Monitor your dietary intake. **Free.**

Games

72. **Candy Crush Saga:** The hit iPhone game encourages you to swipe away candy patterns to complete levels. **Free.**

73. **Temple Run:** The reaction-style adventure game tests your ability to avoid obstacles at speed as you are chased by a gang of angry apes. **Free.**

74. **Cut the Rope:** Get the candy into the Om Nom monster by cutting ropes in this addictive puzzler. **Free.**

75. **Plants vs Zombies 2:** Build up your defences with weapon-firing greenery to protect against armies of marauding zombies reaching your front door. **Free.**

76. **Angry Birds:** Take out all of the pigs by flinging birds with different abilities from a slingshot in this massive mobile hit. **Free.**

77. **The Room**: A suspenseful strategy game, which requires you to unlock puzzles in order to discover supernatural mysteries. **Free.**

78. **Minecraft: Pocket Edition:** The open world-building game allows you to build up the world in your own image. **£4.99.**

Food and Restaurants

79. **Untappd:** Log your favourite beers from around the world, connect with friends and earn badges. **Free.**

80. **Jamie's Recipes:** The Naked Chef gives you the opportunity to subscribe to his latest recipes, packed with photos, videos and helpful tips. **Free.**

81. **Nigella's Quick Collection:** The gastronomic guide includes 70 recipes covering the best comfort foods and video tips of difficult meals. **£3.99.**

82. **Yelp:** Find local restaurants, get directions and read reviews from recent patrons. **Free.**

83. **Big Oven:** Over 250,000 recipes searchable by keyboard. You can enter ingredients you have left in your pantry and see what the app comes up with. **Free.**

84. **Kitchen Pad Timer:** Timers display oven and stove temperatures with an alert to remind you when to take something out. **£1.49.**

To-Do List

85. **Evernote:** Take care of all note-taking from simple to-do lists to recording voice memos, all can be shared and accessed from evernote.com. **Free.**

86. **ToDoist:** Simple yet sophisticated to-do list application, which makes it easier to plan your days. **£0.69.**

87. **Wunderlist:** One of the most attractive and usable to-do list apps on the App Store. **Free.**

Reference and Productivity

88. **Microsoft Office:** Access, create, edit and share Word, PowerPoint and Excel documents. **Free.**

89. **Google Search:** The stand-alone Google Search app for iPhone gives access to Google Now notifications, voice searches, maps, information and more. **Free.**

90. **Forest:** Can't put your phone down? This app helps you focus on work. **£1.49.**

91. **IMDb Movies and TV:** Comprehensive source of information about every film and TV show ever made. **Free.**

92. **Wikipanion:** Wikipanion remembers where you last left a Wikipedia page and keeps a history of all the pages you've searched for previously. **Free.**

93. **Dragon Dictation:** Siri does this also, but Dragon allows you to dictate messages and emails to your phone using voice. **Free.**

94. **Swype:** Making texting a speedier process, swipe across the keyboard to make words with predictive dictionary support to aid accuracy. **£0.79.**

95: **GarageBand:** Create music on your iPhone using a range of digital instruments. **Free.**

96. **1password:** Creates strong, unique passwords for every site, remembers them all for you, and logs you in with a single tap. It also has Touch ID integration. **Free.**

Finances

97. **Mint:** Track your incomings and outgoings and set your monthly budgets. **Free.**

97. **Square Cash:** Send money to friends and family easily. **Free.**

98. **UK Postage Calculator:** Get the right stamps on packages and letters by calculating the price depending on weight and the destination. **£1.99.**

99. **Experian:** Get a free credit report from Experian. **Free.**

100. **Transferwise:** Quickly Send money abroad and avoid huge bank fees. **Free.**

INDEX